100 BIBLE QUESTIONS AND ANSWERS

ANSWERS TO DOZENS OF
BIBLE QUESTIONS AND ISSUES
·
IN-DEPTH RESPONSES TO OBJECTIONS
FREQUENTLY RAISED BY SKEPTICS
·
INSPIRING TRUTHS, HISTORICAL FACTS,
PRACTICAL INSIGHTS

ALEX MCFARLAND
& BERT HARPER

BroadStreet
PUBLISHING

BroadStreet Publishing® Group, LLC
Savage, Minnesota, USA
BroadStreetPublishing.com

100 Bible Questions and Answers
Copyright © 2021 Alex McFarland & Bert Harper

978-1-4245-6350-0 (softcover)
978-1-4245-6351-7 (e-book)

Stock or custom editions of BroadStreet Publishing titles may be purchased in bulk for educational, business, ministry, fundraising, or sales promotional use. For information, please email orders@broadstreetpublishing.com.

Cover images: Preto Perola/Bigstock.com, kwest19/Bigstock.com, Richie Chan/Bigstock.com, Rohan1974/Bigstock.com, Flaviya85/Bigstock.com, Rangizzz/Bigstock.com

Design and typesetting | garborgdesign.com

Printed in the United States of America

21 22 23 24 25 5 4 3 2 1

PRAISE FOR *EXPLORING THE WORD*

I love listening to *Exploring the Word* on my way home from work, and it's a literal blessing to have this book from Pastor Bert and Dr. Alex. I say that because a blessing is something that comes to you, fills your cup, and then overflows to others. Being able to read and study these Scripture-based answers fills me up and then helps me spread the knowledge of God and his Word to the people I interact with daily.

Tyler S., Columbus, OH

Bert and Alex, I have listened to your shows for years and have gained so much practical wisdom. Your insights on Scripture deeply touch my life.

Charles C., Richmond, VA

Exploring the Word has been a part of our daily afternoon drive for many years. Our kids have grown up listening to Alex McFarland and Bert Harper, and our whole family has a knowledge of the Bible thanks to your show.

Erin S., MS

Thank you for your practical wisdom and kindness shown to all callers. You both treat the listeners respectfully—no matter the question—and that really says a lot.

Linda L., Seattle, WA

I don't consider myself a religious person—in fact I'm a bit of a skeptic regarding religion. But I tend to trust what Alex and Bert present on *Exploring the Word*. Not only do they back up their answers with facts, but they also speak with such conviction it is hard not to trust what they say.

Tom B., Chicago, IL

TABLE OF CONTENTS

Section 3: Old Testament Challenges

Section 4: Questions about God

Section 5: Questions about the Holy Spirit

Section 6: Questions about Worldview

Section 7: New Testament Questions

Section 8: Questions about Jesus

Section 9: Questions about Salvation

Section 10: Questions about Sexuality and Gender

Section 11: Questions about Church and Christian Living

Section 12: Questions about the End Times

INTRODUCTION

For more than a decade, we have had the honor of hosting the radio program *Exploring the Word* on American Family Radio. Every weekday afternoon from three to four eastern, we have shared the Bible and have taken thousands of wonderful questions from callers seeking to know God's truth.

Over the years, many have asked us if we have a book with more details about the questions we have answered. This encouragement eventually led us to consider the idea, leading to the book in your hands today. From the numerous thoughts and concerns people have had over the years concerning Scripture, we were asked to address one hundred of the most important questions to help those seeking to better learn about the Christian faith.

The twelve sections you will see in these pages cover everything from creation to the end times. We address issues both ancient and modern, offering biblical truth in brief nuggets to encourage you in your learning. While you can certainly read the book from start to finish, certain questions will likely resonate more deeply with you. We encourage you to look through the table of contents and turn directly to the areas that interest you the most.

We also want to challenge you to share this resource with others. Many Christian books are too detailed to offer as a gift, but this tool has been designed for you to share. Either give your copy to someone when you are finished or, even better, pick up several copies to share with loved ones and friends who want to know more about God. There's even a final "ultimate question" at the end you can use to share the Bible's message of salvation with others.

A couple of cautions before you dive in. First, we have taken on some of the most controversial topics of our time. You might not agree with every conclusion we offer, especially on questions where the Bible doesn't give a direct answer. However, we always look to Scripture as the basis for our decisions and encourage you to do so as well. When we are uncertain of the final interpretation on a difficult topic, we mention that, allowing you to decide from the options we offer as you study.

Second, remember there is a difference between knowing the truth and living the truth. In 1 Peter 3:15–16 we are reminded, "Sanctify the Lord God in your hearts, and always be ready to give a defense to everyone who asks you a reason for the hope that is in you, with meekness and fear; having a good conscience, that when they defame you as evildoers, those who revile your good conduct in Christ may be ashamed."

We are called to know Christ, discover the reasons behind our faith, and put these convictions into action to change our life and the lives of those around us. We don't provide these answers only to increase your knowledge but also to encourage your daily walk with Christ.

We also want to encourage you to communicate with us regarding how this book helps you and to ask other questions you have. You can send us a message through AlexMcFarland.com or email our *Exploring the Word* radio program at word@afa.net.

Lastly, know we are praying for you and look forward to sharing God's Word with you every weekday at AFR.net or an American Family Radio station near you. May God continue to bless your life as you explore the Word!

THE BIBLE

1. WHY DO CHRISTIANS SAY THE BIBLE IS GOD'S WORD? HOW CAN WE KNOW?

The Bible is not only an important book to Christians; it is *the* book. Christians believe the words of the Bible are from God and are, therefore, perfect and important for our lives today.

First, the Bible claims to be from God. For example, 2 Timothy 3:16 pronounces, "All Scripture is given by inspiration from God." Second Peter 1:21 adds, "Prophecy never came by the will of man, but holy men of God spoke as they were moved by the Holy Spirit."

Second, the Bible reveals evidence of being supernatural. How? Look at the prophecies found in Scripture. Hundreds of predictions have been fulfilled in exact detail, from the death of the Messiah in Isaiah 53 to the destruction of Jerusalem and deportation to Babylon in the Old Testament and the prediction of the fall of the Jerusalem temple in AD 70.

Third, the Bible was composed by human writers inspired by God. For example, the first five books of the Old Testament were written by Moses, a man who heard God's voice at the burning bush and on Mount Sinai, where he received the Ten Commandments. David, a man after God's own heart, composed many of the Psalms. The New Testament was written by the apostles and their associates, primarily involving authors who spent time with Jesus during his earthly ministry.

Fourth, the unity of the Bible offers additional support of its divine nature. It includes sixty-six books composed by approximately forty human writers on three continents in three languages over approximately fifteen hundred years. Despite much variety in background, the themes and details of the Bible complement one another as if written by one author. This evidence of a divine author, God, provides supplemental support that its words are truly inspired.

Fifth, the Bible enjoys the evidence of millions of changed lives. While many books have inspired large numbers of people, no book's impact compares with the Bible. Its words have served as the basis for historic documents such as the US Constitution, while its thoughts have been included in countless teachings, plays, poems, songs, and novels.

Sixth, the Bible has shown itself to be a highly accurate historical document. If skeptics could show that Scripture included many historical errors, then the Bible's divine nature could be compromised. However, history and archaeology continue to affirm the accuracy of Scripture, increasing our confidence in its divine origin.

Finally, the Bible's preservation highlights its inspiration. Despite numerous attacks to destroy early copies of Scripture, as well as more recent attempts to burn or ban Bibles, God's Word remains the most translated and distributed book in history. No other book compares to the more than fifteen hundred languages in which the Bible can be read or heard today.

Ultimately, Christians believe the Bible is God's Word based on faith, but it is faith built on facts. The evidence of history, consistency, testimony, and fulfilment all point toward a book that is indestructible and life-changing today.

2. Has the Bible been changed since it was first written?

Many have asked whether the Bible has been changed since it was written. For example, most modern translations include footnotes that mention variations in some manuscripts. Other times, critics claim the Bible is filled with errors because of an alleged difference in a particular copy of the Scriptures. Has the Bible been changed?

In short, the answer is no. Yes, copies of the Bible include some differences, including an occasional important variant, but the text of the Scriptures is essentially the same today as when it was first written. Dallas Seminary New Testament scholar Dr. Daniel Wallace is one of today's top experts on the early manuscripts of the New Testament. When asked about changes in the Bible, he confidently states all the words of the Bible are in the text we have today or in the footnotes. There are no missing books of the Bible somewhere to be discovered in the future.

If the Bible has not been changed, then how do we handle the differences found in the footnotes of our Bible or in the early copies of its manuscripts? Several principles have been developed, but here are a few that we find are most helpful.

First, consider the number of copies of the passage under consideration. For example, if there are ten copies of a book and nine of them are the same, this could point to the one variant being inaccurate and the other nine as accurate.

Second, however, we consider the quality of the copies. In contrast, even if nine of ten readings agree against one that does not, we must look at the context of the single variant. Was the unique reading based on a copy of the Bible that was closer in time to the original text? Does it have historical evidence from other sources to indicate it is to be given more attention? In determining an answer, we don't just count manuscripts; we weigh them.

Third, we compare Scripture with Scripture. We may not be experts on early manuscripts and Bible languages, but we can compare difficult passages with other clear passages for context. If God's Word is perfect, no two passages will directly contradict one another. For example, if one passage says God cannot lie, then we should not find another verse that says God did lie. There is a passage in which God changed his mind in response to prayer, but the context offers insight that shows the event was different from a contradiction in which God lies to his people.

Fourth, the large number of Bible manuscripts from the early generations of the church help us better determine the earliest and original text. For example, if we only had three copies and one was different from the other two, it would be more difficult to tell which copies were original. However, the New Testament has over five thousand manuscripts to evaluate. In the small number of places with meaningful differences, there are numerous options to consider in determining the original reading.

While copies of Bible manuscripts may include some changes, the Bible has not been changed. We can confidently know the Word of God we hold today remains the same as it was given long ago.

3. WHAT DOES IT MEAN THAT THE BIBLE IS "GOD-BREATHED"?

In 2 Timothy 3:16, the apostle Paul said all Scripture is "inspired by God" or is "God-breathed" (NIV). What does it mean to claim Scripture is God-breathed?

The Greek word translated "God-breathed" is *theopneustos*. As you may notice, it includes the words translated "God" (*theos*) and "spirit" or "breath" (*pneustos*). As a compound word, the translation becomes "inspired or breathed by God," emphasizing Scripture as having a divine origin.

In theology, this is referred to as "verbal plenary inspiration." This term indicates inspiration includes the very words of Scripture, not only the meanings they convey.

When Paul wrote these words, he referred to the Old Testament writings. Timothy was from a family with one Greek parent and one Jewish parent. He had been taught the Jewish Scriptures (Old Testament) since his early days through his mother and grandmother (2 Timothy 1:5). In the early church meetings, Timothy was encouraged to preach the Word (2 Timothy 4:1–2) and publicly read it to other believers (1 Timothy 4:13), in part due to lack of access to Scripture and higher levels of illiteracy than today.

To equip and encourage believers, Timothy's call included sharing Scripture. Paul's emphasis on these words as God-breathed noted the power of these words for his young protégé.

Some parts of the Old Testament even refer to God directly inspiring Scripture. For example, God directly gave Moses the laws for Israel, including inscribing words on stone tablets on Mount Sinai. Solomon's words, included in part in Proverbs, are described as from the Lord rather than simply from human hands.

In the New Testament, 2 Peter 1:20–21 describes the writings of the prophets in the Old Testament as being guided by God. The works of Isaiah, Jeremiah, Ezekiel, and others were not a product of their human abilities but were the result of God's Spirit working through them.

One other important biblical passage also highlights the divine nature of the New Testament writings. In 2 Peter 3:15–16, Peter wrote "consider that the longsuffering of our Lord is salvation—as also our beloved brother Paul, according to the wisdom given to him, has written to you, as also in all his epistles, speaking in them of these things, in which are some things hard to understand, which untaught and unstable people twist to their own destruction, as they do also the rest of the Scriptures."

The phrase "the rest of the Scriptures" connects with the writings of Paul—the author of thirteen of the New Testament's twenty-seven books. The New Testament also serves as Scripture, part of the God-breathed writings given by the Lord for our instruction and benefit.

4. WHAT IS THE APOCRYPHA?

The Apocrypha, also known as the Deuterocanonical Books, are included in Catholic Bibles as well as in some Protestant traditions. What are these additional writings? What is their role in the Bible?

The term *apocrypha* means "hidden." These writings were composed during the period between the Old and New Testaments, approximately 400 BC until the birth of Jesus. The names of the included books are 1 Esdras, 2 Esdras, Tobit, Judith, Wisdom of Solomon, Ecclesiasticus, Baruch, the Letter of Jeremiah, Prayer of Manasseh, 1 Maccabees, and 2 Maccabees, as well as some additions to the Old Testament books of Esther and Daniel and Psalm 151.

Interestingly, Jesus and the authors of the New Testament do not appear to directly quote the books of the Apocrypha. There is no indication of these writings as authoritative as in Old Testament quotes that often included "as it is written" or "as Scripture says."

Within the Jewish tradition, these writings were considered important but were not included as part of the Hebrew Bible. For example, the Jewish Talmud excluded these books as a section called *Sefarim Hizonim*, a term meaning "extra or extraneous books."

Largely through this influence, these works were also not incorporated in lists of inspired books by early church leaders. For example, the church leader Jerome is accepted as the person responsible for translating the Bible into Latin for the early church. In his study, he determined the books of the Apocrypha were not divinely inspired and were not to be included as part of the Bible alongside the Old and New Testaments even though the Council of Rome in 382 affirmed these writings.

Though many Catholics accepted the Apocrypha earlier, these books were not added to the Catholic Bible until the Council of Trent in the 1500s in response to the Protestant Reformation.

The Protestant Reformers rejected these books for a variety of historical and theological reasons. It is from these books that some of the unique Catholic traditions arise that Protestants reject, such as praying to saints in heaven (2 Maccabees 15:12–16) or prayers for the dead (2 Maccabees 12:43–45), as well as the tradition popular in the 1500s of giving alms to atone for sins.

Martin Luther's translation of the Bible into German excluded the Apocrypha. However, the original King James Bible printed the Bible with the Apocrypha until 1885 as part of the tradition of the Church of England.

While these and other concerns have rightly led Protestant Christians to conclude the Apocrypha's books should not be included as part of the Bible, they do include important historical information, as well as some helpful wisdom. The book of Ecclesiasticus especially includes statements like Proverbs, while 1 Maccabees offers unique insights into Jewish history that took place between the Old and New Testaments.

We should not accept the Apocrypha's books as the Word of God, but we also do not need to fear them. Instead, we should know the important distinctions between these writings and the Bible and can gain historical perspective through some aspects they provide.

5. WHAT ARE THE GNOSTIC GOSPELS?

The Gnostic gospels are a collection of writing composed primarily between the second and fourth century AD. The Nag Hammadi library includes over fifty titles, with the earliest generally listed as the Gospel of Thomas written in the second century. Though important historical works, these writings are not gospels in the same sense as Matthew, Mark, Luke, and John.

One major difference between these Gnostic gospels and the New Testament Gospels is their time of composition. The four Gospels and other New Testament books were completed during the lifetimes of the apostles and their associates in the first century AD. The Gnostic gospels were written early but in the period after the eyewitnesses of the events had died.

Second, many of the Gnostic gospels were specifically noted as non-biblical or condemned writings by early Christian leaders living near the time they were composed. They are not lost gospels, as some have argued, but are later works known and excluded from the Bible as uninspired writings.

Third, these Gnostic gospels were largely lost to history until the twentieth century. In 1945, the Nag Hammadi library was discovered in Egypt, providing new access to early copies of writings such as the Gospel of Philip, the Apocalypse of Paul, and others. Many of these works had been unknown to modern scholars until this time. In contrast, thousands of early copies of the biblical writings have remained in existence from the time of their writing until today.

While these Gnostic writings are not equal with the New Testament books and are not as early, they are highly valuable for the study of Christian history during the second to fourth centuries, particularly in Egypt and North Africa. These works offer an inside look at what Gnostic writers (those following a philosophy that emphasized enlightenment) believed and taught during this period. Insights regarding language are valuable as well since these documents show how certain words and phrases were used during this early period.

A close look offers insights into many cultural issues and theological concerns emphasized in one region influenced by early Christianity. Through a better understanding of Christianity's early impact, we can perhaps even gain greater understanding for growing in our faith and reaching others today.

6. WHY ARE BOOKS NO LONGER ABLE TO BE ADDED TO THE BIBLE?

Some have wondered if it would be possible for later books to be added to the Bible. However, a close look at Scripture and church history reveals two important reasons this will not happen.

First, the Old Testament was composed during the lives of the early Jewish leaders and prophets. The Hebrew Bible ends with the events of Ezra and Nehemiah about four hundred years before the coming of Jesus, emphasizing the return of the Jews from deportation in Babylon to Jerusalem. Though the Hebrew Bible is listed in a different order and divides its writings into a different number of books (combining the Minor Prophets as well as other sections like 1 and 2 Samuel), it includes the same thirty-nine writings found in our Old Testament today.

Following this silent period, the events of the New Testament took place in the first century AD. The twenty-seven books of the New Testament were all written during this century, either by an apostle or one of their associates (though the authorship of Hebrews is unknown).

Though other early Christian writings certainly existed, these twenty-seven documents were affirmed by the early Christians as the authoritative writings of the church. The early church did not create the list of New Testament books; it simply affirmed them.

Second, the Bible speaks directly against adding to its words. In the Old Testament, Deuteronomy 4:2 says, "You shall not add to the word which I command you, nor take from it." Proverbs 30:5–6 adds, "Every word of God is pure; He is a shield to those who put their trust in Him. Do not add to His words, Lest He rebuke you, and you be found a liar."

In the final book of the New Testament, Revelation also offers a stern warning against adding to or taking away from God's words: "I testify to everyone who hears the words of the prophecy of this book: If anyone adds to these things, God will add to him the plagues that are written in this book; and if anyone takes away from the words of the book of this prophecy, God shall take away his part from the Book of Life, from the holy city, and from the things which are written in this book" (Revelation 22:18–19).

In addition to these two main reasons, the unity of the Bible also reveals its complete nature. God's Word begins in Genesis with the creation of the heavens and earth. It ends in Revelation with the creation of the new heavens and earth. As Jesus taught in Matthew 5:18, "For assuredly, I say to you, till heaven and earth pass away, one jot or one tittle will by no means pass from the law till all is fulfilled."

The phrase "one jot or one tittle" refers to the smallest markings in the Hebrew alphabet. Everything our Lord has given us will come to pass. Nothing needs to be added to it or taken from it. The Word of God is complete, perfect, and continues to change lives still today.

7. HOW DID WE GET THE SIXTY-SIX BOOKS OF THE BIBLE?

The story of the Bible's creation and collection is a fascinating look at God's sovereign work through human history. It includes the thirty-nine writings of the Old Testament and twenty-seven books of the New Testament, each with a unique story, yet united through God's Spirit to impact lives like no other book.

The Old Testament's writings begin with the Law (called the Torah) composed by Moses around 1400 BC. These five books formed the basis of the Jewish faith and nation. The Old Testament also includes books of history (Joshua through Esther), books of wisdom (Job through Song of Songs), and both major prophets (Isaiah through Ezekiel) and minor prophets (Hosea through Malachi).

The Jewish Pharisees in Jamnia are known as the group responsible for affirming our modern list of Old Testament books following the destruction of the Jewish temple in the first century. Their criteria included accepting only books from the writings of Moses to the time of Ezra (1400–400 BC, approximately one thousand years). They rejected the writings of the Apocrypha, accepting the list of writings included in our Bible today.

The New Testament was written in a much shorter period following the earthly ministry of Jesus. Between the '40s and '90s of the first century, some of the apostles and their associates composed writings for early believers that were recognized as authoritative and inspired. These included the four Gospels, written either by an apostle (Matthew, John) or one of their associates (Mark, Luke). Acts chronicles the early history of the church and was the second volume of Luke's Gospel.

The remaining works of the New Testament include thirteen letters produced by the apostle Paul, the general epistles (Hebrews to Jude), and the one book of prophecy by the apostle John, Revelation (likely the last book, composed in AD 95–96). The early church began collecting these works into lists in the second century, partly to determine authoritative works from heretical writings that were beginning to circulate.

These collections were also important due to increased persecution. With Christian writings being destroyed at times, it was vital to clearly indicate which Christian writings were authoritative for the church. Various lists were developed in the second to fourth centuries, leading to the twenty-seven books we have today. Though a few shorter books were disputed by some during the early period as they were not as well-known (such as 2 Peter), Jerome's translation of these twenty-seven writings into Latin for the church made it clear which writings were considered part of the New Testament in the early church.

The Bible we hold in our hands today includes a fascinating history and enormous effort to bring it to us through centuries of transcribing and persecution. Unlike any other book, the Bible is a diverse collection with a single message of the one true God who changes lives still today.

8. WHAT ARE THE DEAD SEA SCROLLS?

The Dead Seas Scrolls were one of the most important discoveries in the history of biblical studies. In 1947, a young shepherd in Qumran, an area about twenty miles east of Jerusalem, threw a rock into a cave and heard it strike a clay pot. When he entered to investigate, he found several pots or jars containing copies of Hebrew texts. Over the next several years, 972 documents from eleven caves would be discovered, including over two hundred Old Testament writings from 300 BC to AD 70.

These writings were, in some cases, more than one thousand years earlier than previously known Hebrew manuscripts! Including at least parts of every Old Testament book except Esther, these materials opened an entirely new world of Old Testament study, allowing scholars to see what the earliest manuscripts looked like during a time much closer to the original writings.

A close investigation of these writings has helped to confirm the high degree of accuracy between these early copies of the Old Testament's writings and later copies. Instead of leading researchers to conclude the Hebrew text had been changed, it largely confirmed the accurate copying of Scripture over a one-thousand-year period.

In addition to the biblical writings found at Qumran, numerous other scrolls have been discovered that have provided insights into the Qumran community. For example, one commentary on Habakkuk provides a look at how early Jews understood his prophecies.

Isaiah was the book with the most copies, perhaps indicating its prominence during the time of Jesus. This would help explain the many references to Isaiah in the Gospels and perhaps even offer a deeper explanation into why Jesus used a reading from Isaiah in the synagogue of Nazareth to reveal his identity as the Messiah.

Historians have appreciated the Dead Sea Scrolls non-biblical writings because of the many insights regarding Jewish culture from this time. From the making of scrolls, to how they were preserved and collected, the observations have provided opportunities to learn about the activities of this unique Jewish movement that existed prior to and during the first century. Some have even suggested the Qumran community includes insights into alternative Jewish movements of the time, similar to the work of John the Baptist who ministered nearby. It's entirely possible John the Baptist served some of those in the Qumran community, though there is no direct evidence of this available.

Another important application of the Old Testament writings at Qumran involves the time regarding when these books were written. Prior to the discovery of the Dead Sea Scrolls, some scholars argued various Old Testament books were written far later than traditionally accepted, in part to explain the accuracy of certain prophecies. However, all the prophecies fulfilled by Jesus now have handwritten copies in existence from before the time he walked on earth, confirming their prophetic nature.

Even seventy years after the discovery of the Dead Sea Scrolls, scholars continue to decipher the many writings found in them for additional insight. Through additional study of these early texts, we continue to better understand God's Word and provide better evidence for the basis of our faith.

9. WHY DOES THE GOSPEL OF MARK HAVE ADDITIONAL VERSES THAT ARE DISPUTED?

A close look at the end of Mark's Gospel reveals footnotes explaining that verses 9–20 of the last chapter are not found in all early manuscripts. Why are these verses disputed?

When the King James Version of the Bible was translated in 1611, access to Greek manuscripts of the New Testament was much more limited than today. Modern scholars can access thousands of Greek manuscripts to better investigate any variations between manuscripts.

Since the translation of the King James Version, two important Greek manuscript discoveries include the Codex Vaticanus and Codex Sinaiticus. Representing the two earliest copies of the New Testament in Greek, both end the sixteenth chapter of Mark's Gospel after verse 8.

In addition, early church writers noted multiple endings of Mark as early as the second century. Between the second century and Jerome's Latin translation of the Bible in the fourth century, a shift occurred from writers arguing for the shorter ending as original to most manuscripts simply copying the longer ending to provide a more satisfactory conclusion to the account.

Because of this history, nearly all other manuscripts of Mark included the longer ending, either alone or with notes of other endings. Because the longer ending is in most manuscripts, many have assumed it must be the earliest ending. However, we do not only count manuscripts; we also evaluate them. Based on the evidence, there is certainly a strong case to be made that the two earliest manuscripts may include the earliest text that ends after verse 8.

Many have questioned how Mark's Gospel could end with the unresolved idea of the women fleeing the tomb in fear. Some have suggested Mark was left unfinished, either intentionally or unintentionally. If intentional, the emphasis may have been similar to the end of Jonah, in which the writing intends to make the reader consider the events rather than providing the full ending to the story. Alternatively, it has been suggested that Mark's book functioned as a set of unfinished notes, with no intention of having a summary at its conclusion.

If the shorter ending was unintentional, this would indicate the original ending was lost. Though unlikely, if the longer ending was added later, it was certainly because it seemed too abrupt in comparison to the other Gospels. In fact, the best explanation for the addition of the longer ending would have been seeing the narrative in need of a final summary to match the other Gospels.

In either case, it has been noted that no major Bible teachings are affected. The one detail not mentioned elsewhere in Scripture is the case of someone drinking poison and not being harmed (Mark 16:18), a tradition some believe may come from an early Christian writing about Philip the Evangelist in Acts.

Though an important matter of research, one's conclusion does not need to alter one's view of Scripture. The longer ending simply affirms details in the other Gospels and Acts and serves to encourage believers regarding the resurrection appearances and the need to share Christ with others.

10. HOW DO WE KNOW WHO WROTE THE BOOKS OF THE BIBLE?

Though God is considered the divine author of the Bible, its writings were composed by human authors. How do we know who wrote the books of the Bible?

The answer is different for each book. For example, the first five books were specifically noted as written by Moses. There is an unbroken chain of witnesses to his authorship that is stronger than any case for the authorship by another writer. For other books, we know the author's name due to external history. For example, in the Gospel of Matthew, the author did not directly name himself in the writing, as the title was added later. However, the early church knew the author and communicated this information accurately.

However, in some cases the author is uncertain. For example, even though many believe Job wrote the book that bears his name, it is possible the account was known orally and written down by someone else. The book is still inspired, but its authorship may be uncertain.

For the Old Testament, Jewish history notes the important role of Ezra. As a priest during the time of the return of Jews to Jerusalem from Babylon, he held an important role in determining which books were authoritative and overseeing those who copied the texts. In the late first century AD, Jewish leaders provided a record of the Old Testament's books, including the thirty-nine we have today along with the authors known at that time. Though authorship was not precisely known for every book, the books had long been established and accepted by this time.

In the New Testament, the authorship of each book is well known except for the case of Hebrews. Many have argued for Paul as the author, but he named himself in all his other thirteen letters. Others have suggested Luke, Barnabas, Apollos, or others. However, the authorship of the work remains somewhat of a mystery. We know approximately when it was written, as it mentions Timothy's release from jail and appears to be during a time of early persecution (likely 64–68), and this anonymity may be explained by the attempt of the author to avoid persecution.

Other books were composed by two or more people. For example, Psalms includes works by several authors. In the New Testament, some of Paul's letters were co-authored works with friends like Timothy, who likely wrote down Paul's dictated words for Paul to review.

In total, the Bible's books include approximately forty authors over more than fourteen hundred years, writing in Hebrew, Aramaic, and Greek. Their backgrounds varied from a fisherman (Peter) to scholars like the apostle Paul. Moses was raised among royalty, while James was raised in Nazareth with Jesus. Luke was a doctor, while Samuel was a prophet from childhood.

However, the origin of Scripture is from the Lord. More than four hundred times, the Bible calls the words of the Scripture the Word of God. This Word proceeds from his mouth (Deuteronomy 8:3; Matthew 4:4). Second Peter 1:21 teaches "prophecy never came by the will of man, but holy men of God spoke as they were moved by the Holy Spirit." From a variety of locations and contexts, God has worked to bring together the world's most amazing book to change our lives and the lives of others.

SECTION 2:

ALLEGED BIBLE CONTRADICTIONS

11. HOW DID JUDAS ISCARIOT DIE? THE BIBLE SEEMS TO PROVIDE TWO DIFFERENT STORIES.

Many have been confused by the differing accounts of Matthew and Acts regarding the death of Judas Iscariot, the disciple who betrayed Jesus. How did he die?

In Matthew 27:5–8, we read Judas hanged himself, his life ending in suicide following his guilt of betraying Jesus:

> He threw down the pieces of silver in the temple and departed, and went and hanged himself.
>
> But the chief priests took the silver pieces and said, "It is not lawful to put them into the treasury, because they are the price of blood." And they consulted together and bought with them the potter's field, to bury strangers in. Therefore, that field has been called the Field of Blood to this day.

However, in Acts 1:18–19, Luke indicates, "(Now this man purchased a field with the wages of iniquity; and falling headlong, he burst open in the middle and all his entrails gushed out. And it became known to all those dwelling in Jerusalem; so that field is called in their own language, Akel Dama, that is, Field of Blood.)" Both accounts share the details of the death of Judas and the Field of Blood but also include unique aspects. Many readers have compared these two passages and concluded they appear to relate two completely different stories.

However, this is not necessarily the case. The order of events was most likely as follows: First, Judas hanged himself in the potter's field. At some point, the rope or branch of the tree he used broke, and his body landed on the ground. His body, either from the fall or later, burst open and left a decaying mess.

Mark and John's Gospels both mention the betrayal by Judas but do not comment on how he died. Therefore, our only information regarding the death of Judas is found in the accounts of Matthew and Luke-Acts.

Luke did not specifically mention Judas hanging himself. Luke's last mention of Judas in the Gospel of Luke includes the moment Judas betrayed Jesus in the garden of Gethsemane. Luke sensed the need to explain what happened to Judas while also explaining how Matthias replaced Judas as an apostle.

Further, Luke mentioned the betrayal by Judas as a fulfilment of prophecy. Acts 1:16–17 most likely refers to Psalm 41:9 that reads, "Even my own familiar friend in whom I trusted, who ate my bread, has lifted up his heel against me." Amazingly, David predicted the very betrayal of Judas approximately one thousand years before it took place.

In reading about Judas and the potter's field, some may wonder who really purchased this piece of land. Was it the priests (Matthew 27) or was it Judas (Acts 1)? Lest any skeptic make more of this than is there, let's point out that there is no necessary contradiction here. Logic tells us that for every effect there has to have been a cause. Philosophers (those among us who often think way too much) use the terms "efficient cause" and "formal cause." Regarding the question of who purchased the potter's field, the priest who engaged in the transaction would have been the efficient cause, but Judas, who threw the twenty pieces of silver on the floor, would have been the formal, or ultimate, cause. So, it is both-and, not either-or.

This same principle is applied to the question of who killed Jesus. Was it the Romans or the Jews? While the Roman soldiers wielding the hammer and spikes may have been the efficient cause, the formal, or ultimate, cause of Christ's death was all of us. We all are complicit with the death of Christ, because it was our sin that put him on the cross. In a world of sinful outcomes, what a blessing it is that God intervened to effect our redemption.

When we compare Scripture with Scripture, we sometimes see two accounts that appear different from one another. However, upon closer look, we can recognize that these differences complement one another and offer a fuller look at the details of á particular event. In this event, the details help us better understand the sweeping magnitude of a fulfilled prophecy from generations earlier. Judas was predicted to betray the Messiah, the prediction was fulfilled, and his end was death.

12. Does Matthew's Gospel mistakenly quote one of Zechariah's prophecies as belonging to Jeremiah?

In Matthew 27:9–10, Matthew says, "Then was fulfilled what was spoken by Jeremiah the prophet, saying, 'And they took the thirty pieces of silver, the value of Him who was priced, whom they of the children of Israel priced, and gave them for the potter's field, as the Lord directed me.'" However, this prediction is not from Jeremiah. It is from Zechariah 11:12 that says, "So they weighed out for my wages thirty pieces of silver." Did Matthew misquote this prophecy?

Researchers have noted at least seven options, including the following:

1. It was said by Jeremiah and later written down by Zechariah.
2. Zechariah's second name was Jeremiah (like "Simon Peter" for Peter).
3. It was a copyist mistake; however, the Syriac and Persian versions have no prophet listed and all the Greek versions do.
4. This is quoting from an apocryphal work of Jeremiah, in the same way Jude quoted from Enoch.
5. Jeremiah actually wrote the last four chapters of Zechariah.
6. Because of a different book order in the Jewish canon, Jeremiah could be given proper credit for any writing of the Minor Prophets.

7. This passage is referring to sections of both Jeremiah and Zechariah, but only Jeremiah is mentioned.[1]

The last two are the most likely options, and both are related. In the Hebrew Bible, their writings include the same thirty-nine books as our Old Testament, but they are divided and ordered differently. The Minor Prophets, for example, are included as one book.

In the time Matthew wrote, the Old Testament prophets were not copied in a book but rather in scrolls. These were often kept in Jewish synagogues and read on the Sabbath for the Jewish community. Rabbis often referred to the first book in a section in reference to the entire section. This could include referring to Jeremiah as a general reference to the prophets.

While this may seem odd to us, we have to keep in mind they did not have chapters and verses like we do today. They could not refer to Zechariah 11:12 to specifically note the verse in mind. In addition, much more focus was on oral tradition. Jewish listeners would hear Scripture in the synagogue and then refer to it as being a reading from the prophets. Understood in its cultural context, this makes the best sense for Matthew referring to Jeremiah in the sense of the prophetic writings, even though the specific verse is from Zechariah.

The other option is that Matthew is emphasizing the potter's field in 27:10. This prophecy is found specifically in Jeremiah 32. In either case, there are ways to understand Matthew's writing that are consistent with the Old Testament rather than contradicting it. Properly understood, these words

---

1   Bodie Hodge and Paul F. Taylor, *Demolishing Supposed Bible Contradiction*: Volume 1, as cited at Answers in Genesis, accessed February 6, 2021, https://answersingenesis.org/contradictions-in-the-bible/mixed-prophets/.

should provide a sense of God's supernatural power to fulfill his words exactly as predicted centuries after being prophesied, strengthening our faith in God and his words today.

13. Why does Matthew 8:5–8 say the centurion came to Jesus while Luke 7:1–10 says the centurion sent emissaries?

Matthew and Luke both communicate the story of Jesus healing the servant of the centurion. Yet some have been concerned about the details of these accounts. For example, Matthew 8 implies the centurion came to Jesus personally, yet Luke says the elders of the Jews came on his behalf. Which is it? Did one of them get it wrong?

There are two possibilities in handling these passages. First, it is possible the elders of the Jews spoke on behalf of their master. Second, the elders and the master were both involved. Let's consider each option.

The first option involves the elders of the Jews speaking on behalf of the centurion. This is certainly possible as servants often had the authority to speak on behalf of a master in Greco-Roman society. If so, the elders of the Jews were the only ones who appeared before Jesus. Perhaps the Jewish-gentile divide kept the centurion from appearing directly before Jesus, sending Jews on his behalf to communicate the message regarding his servant.

This would also make sense because of their emphasis in Luke 7:5 that notes "for he loves our nation, and has built us a synagogue." These Jewish elders were greatly indebted to the generosity of the centurion and would have certainly been willing to communicate on his behalf to Jesus.

It reminds us of when the Bible speaks of Jesus baptizing people. John 4:1–2 says, "When the Lord knew that the Pharisees had heard that Jesus made and baptized more disciples than John (though Jesus Himself did not baptize, but His disciples)…" Jesus is credited with baptizing people though his disciples were the ones directly doing the baptizing. Though we do not usually speak in this manner in our culture, this was very common in the time the New Testament was written.

The second option includes both the elders and the centurion. It is quite possible both the elders of the Jews and the centurion were near one another at the time of this request. The centurion may have believed his request would be better received coming from Jewish leaders rather than from a gentile.

This could also explain how the elders of the Jews, other servants, and the centurion seem involved. Perhaps the elders first made the request, followed by the centurion's servants, and then the centurion himself.

Either option is possible, but it appears the centurion operated indirectly through his servants and the elders of the Jews as Luke described in more detail. As a non-Jew, Luke often described events from the ministry of Jesus in a manner that explained them with more information for a non-Jewish audience (perhaps specifically for his reader, Theophilus in Acts 1:1).

This would best account for Jesus marveling at the message of the centurion as well. If the centurion was not personally there, Jesus would have had a strong reason to be surprised at the faith of a person to send messengers to request a healing from him at a distance. Of course, Jesus responded positively, and he healed the servant in that same hour.

Still today, the centurion's action offers a powerful example for us. When we see others sick or in need, we are likewise called to take their needs to Jesus. As he desires, he can heal in whatever manner he sees fit. He simply calls us to act in faith, bringing our requests to him for his response.

14. Why does Proverbs 26:4–5 say not to answer a fool according to his folly and then say to do so?

Proverbs 26:4–5 says, "Do not answer a fool according to his folly, Lest you also be like him. Answer a fool according to his folly, Lest he be wise in his own eyes." These two verses are exact opposites of one another. How are we to understand these words?

Like many other places in Proverbs, the concepts are parallel to one another to convey a message. In this case, the message highlights that in answering a fool, nothing you say will be taken in a positive manner. In the first verse, if you answer a fool "according to his folly," or in a similar manner to his own remarks, you become like him. This would be like using sarcasm or the fool's style to respond to his foolishness. When you respond in this way, it doesn't help; it only adds to the situation.

In the second proverb, if you answer a fool, it gives him a platform for a response. In other words, giving the fool credibility makes him look wiser than if he were ignored. Instead of improving the situation, it only makes the foolish person look like he or she is at your level.

In either case, the result is negative, and that is the author's point. There is no positive response to a fool's talk. It's trouble if you avoid it and trouble if you address it.

A passage in the New Testament that relates to these proverbs is James 3. James speaks of the power of the tongue, calling it a fire. Though a small part of the body, it can do much damage. As followers of Christ, we are called to rise above the foolishness of the world around us. Instead of using our words for harm or self-focus like a fool does, we are to use our words to share Christ's hope and to build up those around us.

How can we avoid being like the foolish person in Proverbs 26? Ephesians 4:29 teaches, "Let no corrupt word proceed out of your mouth, but what is good for necessary edification, that it may impart grace to the hearers." We must carefully use our words for good. In addition, we must remember God is the one we are to lift up, not ourselves. When we speak of his greatness, it helps keep us from an unhealthy focus on our own accomplishments.

These proverbs are found in the larger context of Proverbs 26:1–12 that highlight the aspects of a foolish person. Verse 1 notes, "As snow in summer and rain in harvest, so honor is not fitting for a fool." Honor is the result of living according to the Lord's wisdom rather than our own.

In verse 12, the conclusion is, "Do you see a man wise in his own eyes? There is more hope for a fool than for him." A person who thinks he is smart is his own undoing. Whether we respond or not, it will not benefit us or the other person. The foolish person's ways are harmful to all.

15. WHY DOES ISAIAH 45:7 SAY GOD CREATES EVIL?

I (Alex) remember one radio program when a caller had read Isaiah 45:7 where God says through the prophet, "I form the light and create darkness, I make peace and create calamity; I, the LORD, do all these things." The caller was curious and wanted to know whether the verse said God created evil.

The question forced me to go back and look at the context of this prophecy. In it, the Lord predicted King Cyrus would subdue nations. God confirmed the accuracy of his prediction by referring to his great power, including the comments in verse 7 of making peace and creating calamity.

Dallas Seminary professor Dr. Thomas L. Constable's words offered help in this verse. He shares:

> The point is that Yahweh alone is ultimately responsible for everything in nature and history. Everything that is in the universe exists because of the creative will of God. God was not claiming that He creates moral "evil" (AV), but both well-being (Heb. *shalom*) and calamity (Heb. *ra'*). He causes (allows) bad things to happen to people for His own reasons (cf. Job 1—2), as well as good things, but He does not cause people to make morally evil decisions (cf. James 1:13).[2]

God affirmed his power for all things in this prophecy. This includes his responsibility for all that takes place under the sun, the good and the bad. However, permitting evil and

---

2   Dr. Thomas L. Constable, "Notes on Isaiah," *Sonic Light* (website), PlanoBible Chapel, accessed February 4, 2021, https://www.planobiblechapel.org/tcon/notes/html/ot/isaiah/isaiah.htm.

causing evil are two different things. God has created humans with the ability to choose right and wrong but does not force us to do right or wrong.

Instead, Adam and Eve were given the choice to obey or disobey God in the garden of Eden. Their disobedience revealed the need for redemption that we experience today through Jesus (John 3:16). Likewise, as fallen humans, we often choose to do wrong. This is not God's fault but rather part of our imperfect sinful nature.

The end of this prophecy notes in verse 13 that God would soon free his exiled Jewish people. This amazing promise was fulfilled as described in the books of Ezra and Nehemiah. Despite seventy years as slaves in Babylon, one thousand miles away from Jerusalem, God provided a way for his people to return and worship him in their land as he had promised.

Still today, the Jewish people remain in the land of Israel. After the Jews lived for nineteen hundred years without a country, the Lord has fulfilled his prediction that they would live in the land in the last days. The Bible even predicts a future Jewish temple that will be desecrated by a global leader prior to the Lord's ultimate return to redeem his people. Just as God fulfilled his promise then, we can live with confidence he will keep every promise until we dwell with him in a new heaven and new earth with all of God's people.

The verse preceding Isaiah 45:7 offers the proper perspective. God says, "They may know from the rising of the sun to its setting that there is none besides Me. I am the LORD, and there is no other." God is unique and the creator of all things. He is perfect, without sin, revealing himself as the one who works through all that occurs in our world to bring forth his righteous plans.

16. Do the Gospels give different accounts of the resurrection of Jesus?

The four Gospels provide four perspectives on the resurrection of Jesus. As four unique writers, their details vary, but some skeptics suggest the writers offer different accounts of Jesus. Is this true?

Not exactly. Just as four eyewitnesses describe the same event with different areas of emphasis and detail, the four Gospels offer a variety of insights for readers that emphasize the overall purpose of their books. For example, Matthew's Gospel heavily focuses on Jewish traditions, offering many details to show how the resurrection connects with Old Testament predictions.

In Matthew 28, for instance, he starts by emphasizing the women going to the tomb after the Sabbath on the first day of the week. Why was this important? In Jewish culture, it was forbidden to work on the Sabbath. Sabbath was from sunset on Friday until sunset on Saturday. Sunday morning was the first time the women could first see the empty tomb.

Mark's Gospel is shorter and more abrupt overall than Matthew or the other Gospels. The shorter conclusion of the Gospel ends with the women running in fear. If original, it leaves readers with an unresolved ending similar to the book of Jonah, where readers must decide what to believe about the empty tomb. The more traditional, longer version of Mark in verses 9–20 include a summary that reflects the traditions found in the other three Gospels.

Luke's Gospel includes insights of interest to his background as a medical doctor. For example, he begins his resurrection narrative with the women and Peter both going to the empty tomb, offering multiple eyewitnesses. Second, he emphasizes the literal resurrection. Luke 24:39 quotes the words of Jesus, "Behold My hands and My feet, that it is I Myself. Handle Me and see, for a spirit does not have flesh and bones as you see I have."

Luke also writes that Jesus ate food, as 24:42–43 explain, "So they gave Him a piece of a broiled fish and some honeycomb. And He took it and ate in their presence." This is something no ghost or spirit would do.

John's Gospel emphasizes his personal retelling of the resurrection. He not only reports what others saw, as Mark and Luke did. He also writes in John 20:8, "Then the other disciple, who came to the tomb first, went in also; and he saw and believed." John personally walked into the empty tomb when Peter was there, and he believed the tomb was empty because Jesus had risen from the dead.

John was also present when Jesus appeared on that first evening (John 20:19) and a week later when he appeared again with Thomas present (John 20:26). Chapter 21 then includes yet another time Jesus appeared to seven disciples with John personally present. In addition to the empty tomb, John writes of three times he saw the resurrected Jesus, personally attesting to the events.

The resurrection appearances do not contradict one another but instead complement one another. We do not need to dismiss them because they include unique details. Instead, we can learn from the information from each Gospel and develop a greater appreciation for the ways Jesus appeared and revealed himself to his followers.

17. WHY ARE THERE TWO DIFFERENT GENEALOGIES OF JESUS?

Matthew 1:1–6 and Luke 3:23–38 provide genealogies of Jesus, but the lists are not the same. Some have even accused these lists of having errors. Why are there two different genealogies?

Several suggestions have been made, but the best interpretation observes that Matthew likely provides the family line of Jesus through his earthly stepfather Joseph, while Luke offers the family line of his mother Mary.

Matthew's focus on Jewish traditions and his connections between Jesus and Hebrew prophecies emphasizes the family line of Jesus through Joseph. Why? He was from the tribe of David, requiring Joseph to leave Nazareth for Bethlehem during a census. This fulfills the predictions of the Messiah coming from the tribe of David, a descendant of Abraham, and explains why the family was in Bethlehem to fulfill the prediction of the Messiah's birth.

Luke's emphasis on Mary in chapters 1 and 2 was likely influenced by eyewitness testimony or early tradition from Mary in the early church (see Luke 1:1–4). He tells of the angel Gabriel appearing to Mary, her visit to Elizabeth, her song of praise, and her view of the birth of Jesus. It would make sense for his genealogy to follow her family background as well.

Rather than emphasizing Abraham and David, Luke, as a gentile (non-Jewish) writer, emphasizes Jesus as coming from Adam, linking him as the Messiah for all people. He also mentions Jesus was "(as was supposed) the son of Joseph," clarifying that Jesus was born of the virgin Mary rather than from Joseph in 3:23.

Are these genealogies important today? Yes, in several ways. First, they reveal Jesus as fulfilling prophecy. Second, they show how the birth of Jesus is rooted in history rather than legend. Third, these generations reveal the many ways God works through unlikely people to fulfill his purposes.

For example, Matthew reveals certain women in his list. Why? He does not include this detail, but Tamar was a Canaanite married to Judah (Genesis 38). Despite Judah's sin, God worked in the life of an unlikely person in the line of Jesus.

Rahab, another woman mentioned in the genealogy, was known as the prostitute who rescued Joshua's spies in Jericho. Though she was not a Jew and lived a sinful lifestyle, her faithful actions led to marrying a Jew and becoming part of the family line of Jesus.

Bathsheba was the woman David married after having an affair with her and having her husband killed. Despite David's sin, God still fulfilled his plan to provide the Messiah through his family line. Ruth was a Moabite yet was known for her faithfulness to her mother-in-law Naomi and to God. She would go on to marry Boaz, and David was her great-grandson. Through these four women, Matthew tells a story of God's work of redemption through the good and bad of humanity to bring forth his plans of the Messiah who would come to offer salvation to all.

Luke also offers much insight, as he includes the account of all humanity and the connection of Jesus to both Jews and gentiles. As a non-Jew, Luke certainly held a deep appreciation for the work of Jesus to offer salvation to all people. He served as a missionary alongside the apostle Paul, offering the hope of salvation and penning the Gospel of Luke (as well as Acts) we use still today.

18. WHY DOES GENESIS 1 SAY ADAM AND EVE WERE MADE AT THE SAME TIME AND GENESIS 2 SAY THE WOMAN WAS CREATED FROM ADAM'S RIB?

Many have noted the differences between the creation of humans in Genesis 1 and 2. However, there is a simple way to understand these differences that does not involve any Bible contradictions. Genesis 1 provides an overall introduction to God's creation of the heavens and the earth. Genesis 2 provides a retelling of the creation account with an emphasis on the creation of the first people, Adam and Eve, in the garden of Eden.

In both chapters, the creation of Adam and Eve occurs on the sixth day (Genesis 1:26–28). Both Adam and Eve were created on the same day, as "male and female He created them" (v. 27). This parallel of male and female reflected the pattern of other animals, made male and female, to reproduce after their own kinds.

In Genesis 2, humans are highlighted as the special creation of God. They are introduced in Genesis 1:27 as made in his image, but Genesis 2 develops the details regarding man's role over the animals and his need for a woman. Adam named the animals, but only Eve was a sufficient partner.

The account of Eve's creation from the rib of Adam highlights a unique aspect of the creation account. No other creature was made in this way. In this exchange, Adam and Eve are shown as interdependent, needing one another and connected to one another in a way only God could design.

This story of Adam and Eve's creation also provides the basis for God's original formation of marriage. Genesis 2:24 teaches, "A man shall leave his father and mother and be joined to his wife, and they shall become one flesh." Just as Adam and Eve were "one flesh" through God's design, husband and wife become one flesh through leaving their parents and forming a new family with one another.

This important origin story of marriage offers many insights for today. For example, God's definition of marriage is one man and one woman committed to one another for a lifetime relationship. This excludes other sexual ethics such as pre-marital sex, adultery, polygamy, or same-sex relationships or marriage.

Interestingly, Jesus affirmed this original design for marriage in responding to a question about divorce in Matthew 19:4–6. Marriage has never been redefined. Though there are examples of other marriage relationships in the Bible (such as Solomon's many wives) and divorce sometimes occurs, the Lord's divine design for marriage remains unchanged. His design should be our goal, and we should seek to preserve marriage whenever possible as part of the unique design of men and women.

Further, this passage provides a clear basis for God's design of humans as male and female. There is no mention of other genders, such as the fifty or more genders sometimes promoted today. While there is no need to belittle or demean those who struggle with gender issues, God is clear regarding the creation of men and women.

These ancient words offer much that remains important still to this day. Genesis 2 offers our most detailed look at the way God created Adam and Eve, offering insights and applications for those who will reflect upon his words today.

19. WHY DOES GENESIS 1 SAY GOD CREATED PLANTS ON THE THIRD DAY AND GENESIS 2:5 SAY "NO PLANT HAD YET SPRUNG UP"?

According to Genesis 1:11–13, God created plants on the third day:

> Then God said, "Let the earth bring forth grass, the herb that yields seed, and the fruit tree that yields fruit according to its kind, whose seed is in itself, on the earth"; and it was so. And the earth brought forth grass, the herb that yields seed according to its kind, and the tree that yields fruit, whose seed is in itself according to its kind. And God saw that it was good. So the evening and the morning were the third day.

However, Genesis 2:5 mentions a time "before any plant of the field was in the earth and before any herb of the field had grown." How could there not be any plants or herbs? Didn't God already create them? Is this a Bible contradiction?

There are two ways Bible interpreters have often understood these two passages. First, Genesis 2 retells the creation story of Genesis 1 with an emphasis on the garden of Eden. God may have simply been restating his steps of creation.

However, there is also a second and perhaps better way to understand the descriptions in Genesis 2:5. The verse does not say there were no previous plants. It only refers to "any plant of the field" alongside "any herb of the field." The emphasis was on a time before Adam and Eve had cultivated plants.

Why was this important? After Adam and Eve sinned in the garden of Eden, their judgment included a curse upon the ground (Genesis 3:17–19). Instead of a lush, fruitful garden that easily provided food for their needs, they would need to work to farm the land for their food.

The account in Genesis 2, therefore, shows the contrast with God providing a place to grow plants for food in the context of his ideal environment, while Genesis 3 reveals how Adam and Eve were forced to work for their food after leaving Eden. Genesis 4 even offers the account of the first murder, as Cain killed his brother Abel over a sacrifice of food when they were in a field.

This account has strong applications for us today as well. God has a plan for our lives, but we can do much harm through our sins. These sins can lead to long-term consequences in our lives and the lives of others. Instead, we are called to obey the Lord and experience his blessing upon our lives.

SECTION 3:

OLD TESTAMENT CHALLENGES

20. WHERE DID CAIN GET HIS WIFE?

Prior to Genesis 4, the only people the Bible mentions on the earth were Adam, Eve, and their sons Cain and Abel. Cain killed Abel and was then judged by the Lord before fleeing to a new land. Then Genesis 4:17 says, "Cain knew his wife, and she conceived and bore Enoch." Where did Cain get his wife?

Though the text does not specifically answer, we can look at the following details. First, God created Adam and Eve as the first people, with Eve being the mother of all the living, according to Genesis 2. Therefore, Cain's wife had to be a descendant of Adam and Eve. In other words, Adam and Eve had other sons and daughters, and one of their daughters (or perhaps one of Cain's nieces) became Cain's wife.

This is also confirmed in Genesis 5. In the genealogy of Adam, the birth of his son Seth is mentioned, with verses 4–5 adding "the days of Adam were eight hundred years; and he had sons and daughters. So all the days that Adam lived were nine hundred and thirty years; and he died."

While incest was later prohibited in the law of Moses (Leviticus 18:6–18), it appears this was a necessity in the early history of humanity. This was also the understanding of Josephus, a first-century Jewish historian, when he retold the history of the Jewish people and early humanity, based on the teachings of rabbis and Jewish priests up to that time.

This mysterious account also informs us that there is much more in the early history of human activity that was not mentioned in the Bible. Scripture provides the essentials for life and godliness, but it does not include every detail of history.

It would be fascinating to know the entire family tree of Adam and Eve and the other first humans, but that was not the goal of Genesis. Instead, the emphasis was on God's creation of people in his image, the story of sin entering the world, the flood, and then on Abraham and his descendants leading to the nation of Israel, God's chosen people, through whom Jesus would come.

It is also important to note the ways the history of Adam and Eve connect with the gospel message. First Corinthians 15:21–22 teach, "For since by man came death, by Man also came the resurrection of the dead. For as in Adam all die, even so in Christ all shall be made alive." Romans 5:17 adds, "For if by the one man's offense death reigned through the one, much more those who receive abundance of grace and of the gift of righteousness will reign in life through the One, Jesus Christ." All humans exist as descendants of Adam and Eve. Likewise, all humans need new life in Jesus Christ.

Our hope in Jesus as the Messiah descended from Adam serves as a vital part of our faith. Cain did not get his wife from some other race or descendants, as such as view would contradict Scripture as well as impact the message of the gospel.

21. WHAT DOES GENESIS 6 MEAN WHEN IT SAYS A MAN'S DAYS WILL BE ONE HUNDRED TWENTY YEARS?

Genesis 6:3 says, "My Spirit shall not strive with man forever, for he *is* indeed flesh; yet his days shall be one hundred twenty years." What does this mean?

Two suggestions are usually made. First, some argue God was judging humanity by limiting the length of human life to one hundred twenty years. However, this seems to be inaccurate, as Noah and many others after him lived to be older than this age. Even today, the oldest human beings have reached over one hundred twenty. While it is true that the length of human life shortened after the time of Noah, this does not prove Genesis 6:3 is speaking about age.

Second, others have understood these words as referring to the maximum number of years until God would judge the earth through the flood during Noah's time. This appears to be the more accurate understanding of the verse.

However, many have misunderstood the one hundred twenty years as the exact number of years until the flood. This is also inaccurate as the ark was built in a much shorter amount of time. Genesis 6:9 reveals God told Noah to build the ark when he already had a wife, three sons, and three daughters-in-law. But Noah was five hundred years old when Japheth was born (Genesis 5:32) and was six hundred when the flood occurred (Genesis 7:6), then the time would have been less than one hundred twenty years.

Japheth, Shem, and Ham were all old enough to have a wife when Noah was given the words of Genesis 6:19. Even if Japheth was married as early as twenty years old and his brother followed this pattern within five years, there could have been no more than seventy-five years between the beginning of the ark's construction and the time of the flood.

Based on the ages of Noah's three sons and the ages at which they married (perhaps between about twenty and forty-five years old), Noah likely built the ark in fifty to seventy-five years. While this indicates Noah and his sons and daughters-in-law all having children at much later ages than in modern times, this timeline best fits the biblical evidence. In fact, the Bible presents people bearing children at much later ages in the generations before the flood, indicating something significant may have occurred during this event that led to shorter lifetimes.

Genesis 11:10 also reveals, "Shem was one hundred years old, and begot Arphaxad two years after the flood." This indicates Shem was about ninety-eight at the time of the flood, two years younger than Japheth. Shem was the second son of Noah, with Japheth the oldest, and Ham the youngest. Genesis 5:27 records Methuselah lived nine hundred sixty-nine years, the oldest age recorded in Scripture. Adding the years of his life until the timing of the flood, he died in the same year the flood occurred. Some have suggested Methuselah even died in the flood, though this is not specifically noted.

We do not have an exact date regarding the time of the ark's construction, but the Bible indicates a timeframe of fifty to seventy-five years is most likely, making it within the one hundred twenty years of Genesis 6:3.

22. HOW COULD THE SUN HAVE STOOD STILL DURING JOSHUA'S BATTLE?

Joshua 10:13–14 reads, "So the sun stood still in the midst of heaven, and did not hasten to go down for about a whole day. And there has been no day like that, before it or after it, that the LORD heeded the voice of a man; for the LORD fought for Israel." How are we to understand these verses? Did God literally stop the sun for a full day?

While commentators have suggested a wide variety of options, there are three main choices: 1) The Bible is wrong, 2) the language is based on appearance rather than a literal stopping of the sun, or 3) God supernaturally changed the timing of the day. Instead of assuming the Bible is wrong (for we believe God's Word is perfect), let's consider the other options.

First, did Joshua write from the perspective of human appearance? In other words, the day felt or looked like a full twenty-four-hour period even if the sun operated as normal. This could be interpreted as the day feeling longer than usual, but the context suggests something more. Some have argued for an eclipse of the sun understood as a sign of God at work in their presence. This could fit the description, as could any natural activity that made the day seem longer, such as a prolonged sunset or refraction of the sun.

Second, some argue that God literally provided a supernatural miracle that stopped the sun. For example, Old Testament scholar Gleason Archer has written:

It has been objected that if in fact the earth was stopped for a period of twenty-four hours, inconceivable catastrophe would have befallen the entire planet and everything on its surface. While those who believe in the omnipotence of God would hardly concede that Yahweh could not have prevented such catastrophe and held in abeyance the physical laws that might be brought to pass, it does not seem to be absolutely necessary (on the basis of the Hebrew text itself) to hold that the planet was suddenly halted in its rotation. Verse 13 states that the sun "did not hasten to go down for about a whole day" (NASB). The words "did not hasten" seem to point to a retardation of the movement so that the rotation required forty-eight hours rather than the usual twenty-four.[3]

However, this is not the only option for those who believe God performed a supernatural miracle. A few years ago, an article by the Royal Astronomical Society journal *Astronomy and Geophysics* argued that the oldest eclipse in history took place on October 30, 1207 BC, suggesting this as the precise date of Joshua's battle.

While difficult to prove for certain, the study provides a scientific basis that supports this biblical event. As with many Bible difficulties, there may be some uncertainty in understanding the passage, but there are ways to interpret the event that remain faithful to God's inspired Word.

---

3   Gleason Archer, *Encyclopedia of Bible Difficulties* (Grand Rapids: Zondervan, 1982), 161.

23. HOW DID GOD CREATE ALL THE WORLD'S RACES OF PEOPLE FROM ADAM AND EVE?

The Bible is clear that God made man and woman, Adam and Eve, in his own image (Genesis 1:27). Eve was called the "mother of all living" (Genesis 3:20). If all people came from these two humans, how do we have so many races or ethnicities of people today?

In addition to all people descending from Adam and Eve, all people also descended through Noah's family that survived the flood on the ark (Genesis 6). People soon built the tower of Babel, resulting in God's judgment through confusing their languages. The Bible uses this account to explain the separation of people into various groups and locations. Genesis 11 includes the table of nations, describing the locations and descendants of Noah's family.

As these groups isolated from one another, certain genetic variations would have become predominant in each group. This would have included characteristics such as height, facial features, hair, and skin tone. Much variation can take place within one generation. Imagine how much variation can take place over several thousand years.

Accepting these variations, however, is not the same as agreeing with evolution. Darwinian evolution claims one species evolved into another over long periods of time. In contrast, variation can take place within a species, but there is no definitive proof of evolution from one species to another.

Modern genetics has helped to show how similar humans are, despite visible difference in skin colors and other traits.

The genetic differences between any two people, regardless of skin tone, is only about one tenth of one percent. It is clear there is only one human race (Acts 17:26).

Even some modern scientific research seems to support the theory that all humans descended from common ancestors:

> In 2004, a computer simulation of life on Earth was created to test and see when the most recent common ancestor for all humans was. The researchers put higher barriers than historically existed to stack the odds against there being a common ancestor in the recent past. Despite this, the results, published in *Nature*, found common ancestors only two or three thousand years ago.[4]

In other words, the most recent DNA studies reveal that today's humans could certainly be connected to common ancestors within a few thousand years. The account of Adam and Eve in the garden of Eden only a few thousand years ago is in no way contradictory to the many characteristics of people living today.

Some genetic studies have also attempted to determine the skin and hair colors of Adam and Eve. However, regardless of these studies, the foundation of Scripture remains the same. Acts 17:26 declares, "He has made from one blood every nation of men to dwell on all the face of the earth."

---

4   T. Wyatt Reynolds, "What Does Science Tell Us about Adam and Eve?" *The Source*, Washington University in St. Louis, June 15, 2020, https://source.wustl. edu/2020/06/can-science-prove-adam-eve-really-existed.

24. WHY WAS CANAAN CURSED FOR HIS FATHER SEEING NOAH DRUNK AND NAKED?

Genesis 9:20–23 includes an odd account of Noah drinking too much wine and becoming drunk. His son Ham found him naked in his tent, and then told his two brothers about the situation. Shem and Japheth responded by walking into their father's tent backwards with a blanket to cover their father so they would not see him in this condition.

Noah later woke up and cursed Canaan, the son of Ham, because of this. Why would Noah respond with a curse?

Some have suggested Ham did something more than simply see his father naked and tell his brothers. However, much of this is mere speculation. The one likely true observation suggests that Ham mocked or made fun of his father Noah when he told his brothers about Noah's nakedness. In contrast, his two brothers did not want to see their father in this condition and respectfully covered their father with a blanket or garment.

The context suggests Ham shamefully reported Noah's nakedness rather than discretely showing respect for his father. But why did Noah curse Canaan instead of Ham? Some have suggested Canaan was involved, but this again speculates about something not found in the text. It is more likely a prophetic statement regarding Ham's descendants through Canaan.

Ham is told, "Cursed be Canaan; A servant of servants he shall be to his brethren" (Genesis 9:25). In contrast, his two brothers receive a blessing. Readers of Genesis during the time of Moses would have quickly recognized this account as the origin and background for the Canaanites, one of their fiercest enemies at the time Moses wrote.

It should also be noted that some have wrongly applied the curse against Ham's family as a form of racial discrimination. Instead of rightly understanding the passage as a prediction about the Canaanites in relation to Israel, some have applied it to Ham's African descendants, with attempts to associate the curse with African slavery and discrimination. This application is biblically inaccurate, historically wrong, and—simply put—racist. There is no biblical support for "the curse of Ham" being applied to any modern group of people.

The account therefore reveals more than one purpose. First, the passage shares insights regarding respect toward parents. Second, the verses provide the background for the enemies of the Israelites with a prophetic background extending to the time of Noah.

Further, the passage's focus on the blessings to Shem and Japheth also point toward these promises being fulfilled through Abraham and later Israel. Canaan would become a servant of Israel, fulfilling an ancient prophecy made by Noah long ago.

Abraham was a descendant of Shem, as noted in Genesis 11:11–26. Abraham would receive the promised blessing of God in Genesis 12:1–3 that would be fulfilled in Isaac, Jacob, and Jacob's twelve sons who would become the tribes of Israel. Through these twelve sons, the nation of Israel would arise, conquering the Canaanites and living as a nation in the promised land. God's amazing ability to fulfill prophecy began very early in human history and continues today. We enjoy the fulfillment of Jesus as the Messiah offering eternal life, yet many additional Bible prophecies still await, including our future hope of eternity with the Lord and his people in a new heaven and earth (Revelation 21–22).

25. WHY DID GOD PUNISH PHARAOH YET BLESS ABRAHAM WHEN HE TOLD SARAH TO LIE AND SAY SHE WAS HIS SISTER?

Genesis 12 shares an account of Abraham (then Abram) telling his wife Sarah (then Sarai) to lie to Pharaoh when they entered Egypt. She was to say Abraham was her brother so he would not be killed and have his wife taken from him. After they entered Egypt, Sarah was taken to Pharaoh's house because of her beauty. But then Pharaoh was punished with plagues. Why was Pharaoh punished when he did not know about Sarah and Abraham's marriage?

A straightforward reading of the passage seems to indicate the judgment was to prevent Pharaoh from taking Sarah as a wife. Verses 18–19 state Pharaoh's words to Abraham, "What is this you have done to me? Why did you not tell me that she was your wife? Why did you say, 'She is my sister'? I might have taken her as my wife. Now therefore, here is your wife; take her and go your way." Further, Pharaoh commanded his men to stay away from Sarah.

The story appears to show an example of God allowing something negative to happen as part of his larger plan. Pharaoh was protected, while Abraham and Sarah were both protected and prospered financially. Though their lying was not approved, God worked despite the situation to protect

Abraham and Sarah to fulfill his promised blessings to them and to their descendants.

Interestingly, the person writing these words was Moses, the leader who freed the Israelites from the hands of another Pharaoh generations later. The account also presents a pattern of God working to protect his people from Pharaoh and his ungodly plans. Moses leading the people from Egypt was not the first time God's people had successfully escaped an Egyptian leader. God would use this event to foreshadow his rescue of Israel.

On another occasion, in Genesis 20, Abraham would use this tactic of lying about his true relationship with Sarah on Abimelech, king of Gerar, a place where his son Isaac would later dwell. Isaac would later also use the same lie with his own wife in Gerar with the Philistines in Genesis 26. In this case, it would serve as the backdrop for the Philistines as the enemies of Israel.

In Genesis 26:28, Isaac's enemies responded, "We have certainly seen that the LORD is with you." An overall takeaway from these events reveals how the nations saw God was with Abraham and his descendants despite their lies and weaknesses. God did not condone their lying, yet despite Abraham's weaknesses (and those of Sarah and Isaac), he worked it as part of his plan for his Jewish people.

These actions serve as a strong reminder of Romans 8:28: "We know that all things work together for good to those who love God, to those who are the called according to His purpose." Such circumstances also note the unstoppable power of God's plans for his people in Jeremiah 29:11: "For I know the thoughts that I think toward you, says the Lord, thoughts of peace and not of evil, to give you a future and a hope."

26. How could Solomon be called a wise man when he had so many wives?

Many have noted the apparent contradiction between Solomon being called a wise man and being a king with one thousand wives and concubines. How could these two factors possibly go together?

Several approaches may be taken to address this question. First, Solomon was called wise long before he began taking multiple wives. Some argue he began with wisdom but later stopped following his own wisdom. For example, when Solomon asked for wisdom instead of money, God answered:

> Because you have asked this thing, and have not asked long life for yourself, nor have asked riches for yourself, nor have asked the life of your enemies, but have asked for yourself understanding to discern justice, behold, I have done according to your words; see, I have given you a wise and understanding heart, so that there has not been anyone like you before you, nor shall any like you arise after you. And I have also given you what you have not asked: both riches and honor, so that there shall not be anyone like you among the kings all your days. (1 Kings 3:11–13)

A second consideration was the purpose of multiple marriages by kings in Solomon's time. Many well-known kings in ancient times were highly regarded for their multiple wives. In the era of Solomon's reign, having many wives was generally associated with having great wealth. Though culturally true, this doesn't make his actions a wise move.

For example, Moses articulated God's commands for future kings in Deuteronomy 17. Verse 17 specifically notes, "Neither shall he multiply wives for himself, lest his heart turn away; nor shall he greatly multiply silver and gold for himself."

A third option is more strategic. Having a wife from a particular nation helped ensure peace with the other nation. In other words, a foreign nation was unlikely to attack when one of its own people was married to the king. Though we do not operate in this way today, Solomon's actions helped to create unprecedented peace for Israel through his variety of strategic marital alliances. According to 1 Kings 11:1, some of his wives included "many foreign women, as well as the daughter of Pharaoh: women of the Moabites, Ammonites, Edomites, Sidonians, and Hittites."

In any case, the Bible called Solomon wise but also revealed his disobedience to God and its consequences. First Kings 11:11 shows the Lord's anger at Solomon's disobedience in serving the gods of his wives: "Because you have done this, and have not kept My covenant and My statutes, which I have commanded you, I will surely tear the kingdom away from you and give it to your servant."

This is an important reminder that many people start well in their faith with God, but few end well. Despite unprecedented wealth and wisdom, Solomon's great kingdom was divided after his death. His sons followed his poor example rather than the godly ways of Solomon's father David. Our relationship with God must be cultivated every day. No one is immune to the effects of sin, whether that of Solomon and his many wives or the temptations we face today.

27. What does it mean that God changed his mind due to the prayer of Moses?

After the Israelites had turned against the Lord and worshiped a golden calf, God told Moses, "I have seen this people, and indeed it is a stiff-necked people! Now therefore, let Me alone, that My wrath may burn hot against them and I may consume them. And I will make of you a great nation" (Exodus 32:9–10).

However, Moses prayed and pleaded with the Lord to spare the people. In verse 14, we are told, "So the LORD relented from the harm which He said He would do to His people." What does it mean that God changed his mind?

This may be a difficult passage, but it is not impossible to understand. First, we must recognize that God knows all things, from eternity past to eternity future. There is nothing that surprises him. He knew the people would rebel against him. He also knew Moses would intercede to spare them. The only reasonable conclusion, then, is that the Lord made this statement to hear the response of Moses.

God does not have a "mind" in the same sense as humans that changes upon request. He already has a plan in place. Though our prayers matter and do make a difference, we are to pray according to his will that includes him knowing all future activities. He does not change his mind due to our prayers; he accomplishes his will through our prayers.

The same was true in the life of Moses. He asked the Lord for mercy, and the Lord said yes. However, God's answer was not completely positive. Many people died in the resulting judgment, revealing the powerful consequences of sin and turning from the Lord.

Another important issue in this passage is the Lord's reference to making Moses into a nation of his own. The words are very similar to God's words to Abraham in Genesis 12:2, in which he promised to bless Abraham and make him into a great nation. These words would have reminded Moses of the past promise to Abraham, leading to his response to, "Remember Abraham, Isaac, and Israel, Your servants, to whom You swore by Your own self, and said to them, 'I will multiply your descendants as the stars of heaven; and all this land that I have spoken of I give to your descendants, and they shall inherit it forever'" (Exodus 32:13).

In this manner, God used the circumstances to remind Moses of his promise he would fulfill through Abraham and the tribes of Israel. He could not and would not destroy them but would bring them into the promised land despite their weaknesses and failures. This powerful story serves as a reminder to us today as well. We often fail the Lord through our actions, yet he remains faithful to us. Despite our weaknesses, his love for us provides redemption and salvation, ultimately leading to eternal life for all who believe (John 3:16).

28. How could God harden Pharaoh's heart?

It seems rather odd that God would punish Pharaoh with plagues if he was the one who hardened Pharaoh's heart (Exodus 10:20, 27; 11:10). How is this fair?

First, Exodus notes that God hardened Pharaoh's heart and that Pharaoh hardened his own heart (Exodus 8:15, 32; 9:34). This is not a conversation about a godly man God turned bad but rather an ungodly leader God controlled to accomplish his purposes.

Remember, this is a leader who enslaved well over one million Jews and kept them under the nation's control for four hundred years. This is also the same nation that killed infant sons among the Jews to control the population and keep the Jews under their power. God's "hardening" did not change a good Pharoah to a bad Pharaoh but rather directed his choices toward God's impending judgment for his evil actions.

Second, this hardening of Pharaoh's heart served as part of the fulfilling God's greater plan for his Jewish people. Romans 9:17–18 says, "For the Scripture says to the Pharaoh, 'For this very purpose I have raised you up, that I may show My power in you, and that My name may be declared in all the earth.' Therefore He has mercy on whom He wills, and whom He wills He hardens."

Third, Pharaoh was given many opportunities to obey God's commands through Moses. God sent ten different plagues, each increasing in power and judgment to convince Pharaoh of God's supremacy. Even after the death of his first-born son, Pharaoh soon changed his mind about letting the

Israelites go, and he chased them to the Red Sea. He would not stop until his army was destroyed in a devastating finale by the judgment of water overtaking his forces.

From a human perspective, it may appear as if God is not fair when he hardens someone's heart. However, Scripture is clear that "all have sinned and fall short of the glory of God" (Romans 3:23). From Pharaoh to our own selves today, we all stand in need of the grace of the Lord.

In addition, God always has a greater plan at work in the world around us. We do not know why some receive Christ and others reject him. However, we do know he desires all people to know the truth of the gospel, and he calls us to make disciples of all nations (Matthew 28:18–20). We are called to sow the seed of the gospel while he determines how the seeds grow. As Paul wrote, "I planted, Apollos watered, but God gave the increase. So then neither he who plants is anything, nor he who waters, but God who gives the increase" (1 Corinthians 3:6–8).

Finally, we realize that God allows everyone some degree of understanding about the Creator. We are not innocent people who have no knowledge of our maker. We are people who know what is right and often choose wrongly. Romans 1:20 teaches, "For since the creation of the world His invisible attributes are clearly seen, being understood by the things that are made, even His eternal power and Godhead, so that they are without excuse." Apart from the saving power of Jesus, we are all under judgment.

29. Why did God punish David for taking a census of Israel?

When David was king of Israel, he commanded a census to be taken of the people. Why did God punish him for doing this?

Two passages speak of the motives concerning this event. First Chronicles 21:1 says, "Now Satan stood up against Israel, and moved David to number Israel." But 2 Samuel 24:1 says, "Again the anger of the Lord was aroused against Israel, and He moved David against them to say, 'Go, number Israel and Judah.'"

These accounts seem to contradict one another. Was it the Lord or Satan leading David to take a wicked census? First Chronicles identifies Satan as the motivator, but 2 Samuel blames the event on the anger of the Lord. The use of "Again" seems to refer to the one other time the anger of the Lord is noted in 2 Samuel 6:7. There, Uzzah touched the ark of the covenant and died. What was similar in both passages? David chose to do something in a manner God had not commanded. The anger of the Lord seems to be the consequence of the action not the motive for it.

This would certainly make more sense of the following actions. For example, if Satan was the tempter and the anger of the Lord was the consequence, we can easily see the relationship between temptation, sinful action, and judgment. Kings counted their people to measure their power. It served as a source of pride. This pride is the same temptation Satan gave to Jesus when he offered our Lord all the kingdoms of the world if Jesus would bow to him (Matthew 4:9).

After the census, the Lord convicted David of his sin. He said to the Lord, "I have sinned greatly in what I have done; but now, I pray, O LORD, take away the iniquity of Your servant, for I have done very foolishly" (2 Samuel 24:10). The Lord sent the prophet Gad with three options from which to choose, with David choosing to fall into the hands of God rather than his enemies. Seventy thousand people died in the resulting judgment (v. 15).

As part of God's larger plan, David purchased the land where the judgment stopped. David built an altar in that location where he presented an offering and prayed to God. This would become the future location of the Jewish temple. Though currently destroyed, God even predicts this temple will one day stand again in the end times, with a millennial temple mentioned in Ezekiel (40–48) where the Lord will reign (Revelation 20:1–6).

God's plans often do not make sense to us at the time they occur. However, his ways are higher than our ways: "For as the heavens are higher than the earth, so are My ways higher than your ways, And My thoughts than your thoughts" (Isaiah 55:9). God does not tempt us (James 1:13), but when we sin, God's anger is revealed, and judgment may result. We stand in need of a Savior who can forgive our sins and redeem us from judgment. We are called to confess our sins, for "If we confess our sins, He is faithful and just to forgive us *our* sins and to cleanse us from all unrighteousness" (1 John 1:9).

30. WHAT MARK DID GOD GIVE TO CAIN?

In Genesis 4:15 we read, "The LORD set a mark on Cain, lest anyone finding him should kill him." However, the account does not tell what the mark was. What mark did God give to Cain?

While this mark is not specifically mentioned, we can discover some information through study of the Scriptures. The other places the word translated "mark" is used generally refer to an external marking, such as tattoo. This may indicate some kind of scar or external marking visible to all who would have seen Cain.

It should be noted that some people have wrongly sought to connect the mark of Cain with dark skin, associating the mark of Cain with attempts to justify racism. There is no indication of this interpretation in the Bible, and it is to be firmly rejected. God created all people in his image (Genesis 1:27), and we are called to treat all people with love and respect.

Others have suggested the mark on Cain was not physical but an invisible or symbolic mark. While possible, there is no clear way to determine what the meaning of a symbolic mark might be.

However, it is interesting to see how markings are used throughout the Bible. For example, Ezekiel was commanded to place a mark on the heads of certain people (Ezekiel 9:4). In the end times, the mark of the beast will be placed on people as a sign of their control by the future global Antichrist (Revelation 13). A marking is generally a symbol of control. In Cain's case, whatever mark he had showed the control God had over his life, keeping others from killing him.

This mark also served as a sign of mercy from judgment, keeping Cain from the punishment he rightly deserved for killing his own brother. In the New Testament, Paul similarly talks about the way the Holy Spirit seals us: "Now He who establishes us with you in Christ and has anointed us is God, who also has sealed us and given us the Spirit in our hearts as a guarantee" (2 Corinthians 1: 21–22).

Ephesians 1:13–14 adds, "In Him you also trusted, after you heard the word of truth, the gospel of your salvation; in whom also, having believed, you were sealed with the Holy Spirit of promise, who is the guarantee of our inheritance until the redemption of the purchased possession, to the praise of His glory." Ephesians 4:30 also instructs, "Do not grieve the Holy Spirit of God, by whom you were sealed for the day of redemption."

We may not be able to fully explain Cain's mark, but it is certainly filled with meaning for us today. Just as the Lord protected him with a mark to seal him from the judgment of other people, the Lord has sealed us by his Holy Spirit as believers to protect us from future judgment as we live as strangers in this world on our way to be at home in the Father's house.

31. WHY DID GOD FLOOD THE WORLD DURING NOAH'S TIME BUT DOESN'T FLOOD THE EARTH TODAY?

God clearly states why he flooded the earth during Noah's time:

> Then the LORD saw that the wickedness of man was great in the earth, and that every intent of the thoughts of his heart was only evil continually. And the LORD was sorry that He had made man on the earth, and He was grieved in His heart. So the LORD said, 'I will destroy man whom I have created from the face of the earth, both man and beast, creeping thing and birds

of the air, for I am sorry that I have made them.'" (Genesis 6:5–7)

God destroyed the earth due to the wickedness of people. He chose to restart the earth's spread of humanity through Noah, a person who found "grace in the eyes of the LORD" (Genesis 6:8), and his family. However, this does not explain why the earth is not flooded today. People continue to sin, and wickedness certainly remains. Why doesn't God send another flood today?

The answer is found after the flood in Genesis 9:11. The Lord promised not to destroy the earth again by water, saying, "Thus I establish My covenant with you: Never again shall all flesh be cut off by the waters of the flood; never again shall there be a flood to destroy the earth." God gave the sign of a rainbow, offering a vivid symbol of hope to remind all people of God's protection despite his judgment of sin.

The apostle Peter refers to the flood as a symbol of God's salvation: "In the days of Noah,...the ark was being prepared, in which a few, that is, eight souls, were saved through water. There is also an antitype which now saves us—baptism (not the removal of the filth of the flesh, but the answer of a good conscience toward God), through the resurrection of Jesus Christ" (1 Peter 3:20–21). The water of the flood serves as a type of what we see in baptism. In baptism, our goal is not removal of dirt but the symbol of a new life of faith in Jesus.

Instead, 2 Peter 3:5–7 foretells how God will judge the world in the future, not with a flood, but with fire: "For this they willfully forget: that by the word of God the heavens were of old, and the earth standing out of water and in the water, by which the world that then existed perished, being flooded with water. But the heavens and the earth which are now preserved by the same word, are reserved for fire until the day of judgment and perdition of ungodly men."

After this judgment, we will ultimately experience a new heaven and earth where all God's people will dwell with him forever. God's judgment has not ended, but judgment through a global flood has. This one-time event brought devastating consequences upon the earth but does not compare to the future judgment that will require a new heaven and earth.

32. HOW COULD GOD PERMIT THE DEATH OF ACHAN'S ENTIRE FAMILY FOR HIS SIN?

In Joshua 7, Achan and his entire family are put to death for his sin of keeping some of the items from the destruction of Jericho. Why did God command his entire family to be put to death?

First, let's look at the command. In Joshua 6:18 says, "And you, by all means abstain from the accursed things, lest you become accursed when you take of the accursed things, and make the camp of Israel a curse, and trouble it." Joshua proclaimed God's curse on anyone who kept items from the battle of Jericho.

The Israelites defeated Jericho and moved to the next city called Ai. They were surprisingly defeated, with thirty-six men killed and the people fearing for their lives. The Lord revealed to Joshua the defeat was due to the sin of someone from among their people.

After Achan was caught, he admitted to his wrong: "When I saw among the spoils a beautiful Babylonian garment, two hundred shekels of silver, and a wedge of gold weighing fifty shekels, I coveted them and took them. And there they are, hidden in the earth in the midst of my tent, with the silver under it" (Joshua 7:21). In judgment, Achan, his family, and even his livestock and belongings were destroyed.

But why kill his family? We are not given much detail, but it is clear that God had promised a curse on anyone who broke his rule in this area. This curse resulted in the death of Achan and those with him.

Second, it is likely his family was aware of his crime and may have helped him. Achan's family members would have known about a hole dug in the middle of their tent where he buried the items. Instead of turning him in, they remained silent. They were guilty for their role in the wrongdoing as well.

Third, their actions led to the deaths of thirty-six Israelites. This was not only a theft that disobeyed God, but it was also an action that was responsible for the lives of several of their people. Capital punishment was a reasonable action from their perspective in this matter.

A similar consequence is found in the account of Korah's rebellion in Numbers 16. Despite Korah being the leader of the rebellion, his entire family was destroyed. It appears their support of his rebellion was sufficient to draw God's judgment. Both examples reveal that a person does not have to lead in sinning to receive judgment; we are also called to oppose others who do wrong even when it involves members of our own family.

These actions are an example of Proverbs 15:27, which teaches, "He who is greedy for gain troubles his own house." Another example is found in Proverbs 1:19: "So are the ways of everyone who is greedy for gain; It takes away the life of its owners." Greed is a sin that leads to personal harm as well as harm to one's family.

33. DID GOD CONDONE RAHAB'S LIE?

In Joshua 2, Joshua's two spies to Jericho were being pursued by their enemies. They hid in the home of Rahab. In verses 4–5, she lied to the officers, saying, "Yes, the men came to me, but I did not know where they were from. And it happened as the gate was being shut, when it was dark, that the men went out. Where the men went I do not know; pursue them quickly, for you may overtake them."

In the following verses, she expressed her faith in (and fear of) the God of Israel, asking the two spies she had hidden on her roof to spare her when they later attacked the city. The Israelites did spare her. Does this mean God condoned her lie?

God opposes lying, listing it as one of the Ten Commandments. However, in this specific case, her lie saved the lives of God's people. Her choices were to allow murder or to lie, two sins listed in the law of God. She chose the option that saved lives, and God honored her choice.

In addition to detailing the sparing of Rahab's life, the New Testament offers three important insights into her life. First, Rahab is listed in Matthew 1:5 as the wife of Salmon and mother of Boaz. Boaz married Ruth, from whom David and later Jesus were descended. Her faithfulness was even honored by becoming part of the family line of Israel's most famous king and the Messiah!

Second, Hebrews 11:31 mentions Rahab in the list of faithful people of the Old Testament: "By faith the harlot Rahab did not perish with those who did not believe, when she had received the spies with peace." She blessed God's people by saving their lives. God blessed her for saving others, despite misleading soldiers to do so.

Third, James 2:25 says, "Likewise, was not Rahab the harlot also justified by works when she received the messengers and sent them out another way?" Her action was noted as a righteous work as it saved the lives of God's people.

While we may never face a life and death situation like Rahab did, God's Word is clear that protecting life is top priority. During the Holocaust in Nazi Germany, Rahab's story was echoed in a very important way. In some cases, Christians were placed in situations in which they hid Jews and were forced to lie or deceive to keep them from being sent to a concentration camp or being outright killed. History remembers such people today as what Jews call "the Righteous," non-Jews who saved lives during the Holocaust.

Rahab's example shows the tremendous value of life and that extreme situations sometimes require choices not normally condoned. We should not look at her example as an excuse to lie when it is to our convenience. Her choice was certainly not convenient for her, and it could have resulted in her own death. While lying is wrong, saving innocent lives is of utmost importance.

34. WHAT DOES IT MEAN WHEN THE BIBLE SAYS MAN HAS BECOME LIKE GOD?

At the end of God's judgment upon Adam and Eve, Genesis 3:22 states, "Behold, the man has become like one of Us, to know good and evil. And now, lest he put out his hand and take also of the tree of life, and eat, and live forever." What does it mean that man has become like one of us?

It is significant that God speaks of "Us." Why would God refer to himself in the plural? There are three options. First, some suggest God is speaking with the heavenly angels. In this interpretation, the angels are the "Us."

Second, others have suggested the usage resembles the ancient tradition of kings speaking of themselves in plural form. This is generally the Jewish understanding of the passage since Jews do not believe in Jesus as the Messiah or in the Trinity.

Third, many see this as an early reference to the Triune nature of God. The "Us" is Father, Son, and Holy Spirit, all three persons of the Godhead communicating with one another. While any of these views is possible, this third view is preferred.

But this still does not answer what it means for Adam and Eve to become like God. The context of the verse best addresses this aspect of the question. It tells us the way they have become like God is in knowing good and evil. Prior to sinning in the garden of Eden, Adam and Eve had never known evil. After being tempted by the serpent (Satan), they discovered evil, opening a new area of understanding, just as God knew about good and evil.

Interestingly, God removed Adam and Eve from the garden of Eden to keep them from eating of the tree of life and living forever. Their judgment included death. The Bible teaches elsewhere the wages (or result) of sin is death (Romans 6:23).

However, the tree of life is mentioned again in Scripture. Proverbs mentions the tree of life four times a symbol of life. Revelation mentions the tree of life literally. Revelation 2:7 says, "To him who overcomes I will give to eat from the tree of life, which is in the midst of the Paradise of God." The tree of life is now in "Paradise" or heaven.

Revelation 22:2 specifically mentions the tree of life is located in the new heavens and earth: "In the middle of its street, and on either side of the river, was the tree of life, which bore twelve fruits, each tree yielding its fruit every month." Those who live near this tree of life are those who will spend eternity with God.

Finally, Revelation 22:14 says, "Blessed are those who do His commandments, that they may have the right to the tree of life, and may enter through the gates into the city." This future heavenly city, the heavenly Jerusalem, will be the home of God's people who will one day eat from the tree of life. We will then become like God in the sense that we, too, will experience eternal life.

35. HOW CAN GOD BOTH PUNISH THE GUILTY AND FORGIVE THE WICKED IN EXODUS 34?

Following the judgment upon the Israelites for worshiping the golden calf, God sent Moses to Mount Sinai a second time to receive a new copy of the law. When the Lord descended in the cloud to meet with Moses, he said, "The LORD, the LORD God, merciful and gracious, longsuffering, and abounding in goodness and truth, keeping mercy for thousands, forgiving iniquity and transgression and sin, by no means clearing the guilty, visiting the iniquity of the fathers upon the children and the children's children to the third and the fourth generation" (Exodus 34:6–7). How can God both punish the guilty and forgive them?

The answer is found in the response of Moses in verse 9: "If now I have found grace in Your sight, O LORD, let my LORD, I pray, go among us, even though we are a stiff-necked people; and pardon our iniquity and our sin, and take us as Your inheritance." God forgives those who humble themselves before him, yet he punishes those who refuse him.

The following verses contrast God's work in the lives of the Jewish people with the ways of the people in the land they would inherit where other gods were worshiped. These people would be punished, in part through God giving the land to his people in fulfilment of his promises to Abraham and Moses.

The passage concludes with Moses receiving the Ten Commandments to take back to the people of Israel. They were expected to know God's truth and to obey it by faith to experience God's forgiveness as they journeyed toward the promised land.

This verse is part of a larger theme in the law of Moses that frequently called God's people to obey him and flee from sin to receive his blessing and escape his judgment. God gave a covenant to his people through Moses that prohibited them from making a covenant with the people of the land who followed other gods.

Today, we live under the new covenant in the grace of Jesus Christ. Rather than the law of Moses (though still inspired and of tremendous value), we focus our lives on salvation in Christ and living by faith through the power of God's Spirit in our lives. First John 1:9 teaches, "If we confess our sins, He is faithful and just to forgive us our sins and to cleanse us from all unrighteousness."

In contrast, those who reject faith in Jesus Christ will receive eternal punishment. Matthew 25:46 warns, "These will go away into everlasting punishment, but the righteous into eternal life." Matthew 10:28 adds, "And do not fear those who kill the body but cannot kill the soul. But rather fear Him who is able to destroy both soul and body in hell." We don't like to talk about the eternal punishment of hell, but God's Word is clear that those who reject Christ will not experience his forgiveness; they will experience his judgment.

SECTION 4:

QUESTIONS ABOUT GOD

36. IF GOD MADE EVERYTHING, WHO MADE GOD?

Many have asked, "Who made God?" It is a natural thought to consider upon recognizing God's creation of all things. If everything else is made by God, shouldn't God have an origin as well?

The study of this question has led philosophers to sometimes call God the First Cause. While it is true all created things came from something, a first cause is necessary as the origin of all things. In other words, everything cannot come from nothing. If you ask, "Who created God?" then you could continue to ask, "Who created the one who created God?" and on and on without end.

Instead, the Bible simply begins with the words of Genesis 1:1 that, "In the beginning, God created the heavens and the earth." It assumes a beginner, Creator, or First Cause as the basis for the rest of creation.

Colossians 1:16–17 includes insight regarding the role of Jesus in creation: "For by Him all things were created that are in heaven and that are on earth, visible and invisible, whether thrones or dominions or principalities or powers. All things were created through Him and for Him. And He is before all things, and in Him all things consist." As the second person of the Triune God, Jesus was involved in everything in creation. He likewise sustains all things, offering an explanation both for creation and the continued existence of our universe.

Interestingly, modern science points to the common need for a creator. The theory of the Big Bang as the origin of time, space, and matter requires a creator. Even those who suggest the idea of multiple universes cannot escape the need for an original starting point rather than a past extending into eternity.

Today, many refer to this First Cause as an Intelligent Designer. Why? The original cause of our universe includes a massive amount of intelligence as well as intricate design. The most recent research even points increasingly against Darwinian evolution as a sufficient answer for living things—including humans—as the complexity involved in a single cell is much greater than previously known.

While most philosophers and even scientists will admit the necessity of a First Cause or Intelligent Designer, not everyone wants to agree that this starting point is the God of the Bible. However, our Christian faith affirms both God's creation and his involvement in creation. Most importantly, this includes God himself leaving heaven for earth through Jesus Christ, offering the ability for those who believe to become a new creation in him.

Second Corinthians 5:17 reminds us, "If anyone is in Christ, he is a new creation; old things have passed away; behold, all things have become new." Galatians 6:15 adds, "For in Christ Jesus neither circumcision nor uncircumcision avails anything, but a new creation." We live in a universe created by God and can become a new creation through Christ, living with the Holy Spirit within us today.

37. HOW CAN ANYONE KNOW WHAT GOD IS LIKE?

As limited human beings, how can we know anything about God? How can we understand what God is like? These questions have long been given attention throughout history. In Acts 17, the Greeks in Athens had many gods, including an altar to an "unknown god." The apostle Paul claimed to make the unknown God known, offering the message of hope in Jesus Christ.

As finite people, we cannot know everything about God, but that does not mean we are unable to know anything about him. But what areas can we know information about God? Scripture mentions four main ways: conscience, creation, Scripture, and Christ.

In Romans 2:15, we are told every person has a certain amount of awareness of God, and they "show the work of the law written in their hearts, their conscience also bearing witness, and between themselves their thoughts accusing or else excusing them." In this context, Paul reveals every person has some understanding of a higher power or maker beyond them.

Second, Romans 1:20 states that creation reveals certain information about the creator: "For since the creation of the world His invisible attributes are clearly seen, being understood by the things that are made, even His eternal power and Godhead, so that they are without excuse." Paul says people are without excuse since creation is available to all people to "read" as evidence regarding the maker of heaven and earth.

Third, Scripture offers God's revealed words to provide specific information about God. Second Timothy 3:16–17 calls Scripture inspired ("God-breathed," as the NIV has it), while many places throughout the Bible refer to it as the words of God. Psalm 119, the longest chapter in the Bible, affirms the power and wisdom of the Scriptures, offering wisdom, freedom from sin, and information for eternal life.

Fourth, Christ coming to earth offered a powerful example of what God is like. He was human, yet he lived without sin (Hebrews 4:15). He showed himself as a great teacher, healer, and miracle worker, and he had power over Satan, demons, and even death.

John 1:1–4 offers a compelling picture of Christ's role in showing what God is like: "In the beginning was the Word, and the Word was with God, and the Word was God. He was in the beginning with God. All things were made through Him, and without Him nothing was made that was made. In Him was life, and the life was the light of men." Jesus was noted as creator, Triune, equal with God, and the one who gives light. This summary of Jesus provides clear information regarding the God who made us and desires to know us personally.

Conscience, creation, Scripture, and Christ offer much insight into what God is like. Scripture provides the most specific information, showing us the need to study the Bible today to better know our Lord. Yet we must believe in Christ to truly know God and his love for us, which offers us abundant life today and eternal life in the future.

38. SINCE GOD CAN DO ANYTHING, CAN GOD EVER SIN?

Matthew 19:26 tells us all things are possible with God. But if God can do anything, can he sin? If so, he would not be a perfect God. If not, he is limited and is not God. This is an apparent contradiction many skeptics have used in attacking God's existence or definition. However, in the case of God, his perfection provides positive limitations that keep him from doing anything wrong or anything he does not desire to do.

Yes, God can do anything, but we must recognize that God can do anything that is according to his will. Since God is perfect, he has no desire to sin and therefore will not sin and cannot sin. Hebrews 4:15 speaks of Jesus as being like us, taking on human form, yet not sinning. He resisted the temptations of Satan in ways people cannot, proving himself to be greater than any spiritual enemy and perfect in all ways.

First John 3:5 specifically says God the Son, Jesus Christ, cannot sin: "You know that He was manifested to take away our sins, and in Him there is no sin." He has never sinned in the past and cannot sin in the future.

James 1:13 also teaches, "God cannot be tempted by evil, nor does He Himself tempt anyone." First Peter 2:22 adds Jesus is the only one "who committed no sin, nor was deceit found in His mouth." God is both sinless and does not tempt anyone else to sin. Sin is part of our imperfect, fallen nature as humans that allows us to choose wrong in contrast with God's perfection.

Further, the fact of God's many attributes of holiness, perfection, and purity keep him from being able to do anything wrong. He knows all things, including any temptation, and is therefore unable to do wrong.

The fact that God is unable to sin is of great benefit to us. First Peter 3:18 teaches, "For Christ also suffered once for sins, the just for the unjust, that He might bring us to God, being put to death in the flesh but made alive by the Spirit." His righteousness makes it possible for us to be forgiven and have eternal life. John 3:16 adds, "For God so loved the world that He gave His only begotten Son, that whoever believes in Him should not perish but have everlasting life." God's perfect love covers over our sins and offers us eternal life as well.

Why is this important? An article from the Billy Graham Evangelistic Association explains:

> It's important for one reason: Only someone who was without sin could save us from our sins. And that is what happened when Jesus died on the cross: All our sins were transferred to Him, and He took upon Himself the judgment we deserve. Don't carry your burden of sin and guilt any longer, but open your heart to Jesus Christ and trust Him alone for your salvation.[5]

---

5 "Did Jesus Ever Commit Sin?" Billy Graham Evangelistic Association of Canada, accessed February 8, 2021, https://www.billygraham.ca/answer/did-jesus-ever-commit-sin/.

39. WHAT DID GOD DO BEFORE THE CREATION OF THE UNIVERSE?

Even many Christians wonder what God did before creating the heavens and the earth. From speculation that God was creating other universes to stories of cosmic battles, many theories exist.

However, Scripture is clear that God *is* the beginning and the end. Jesus said, "I am the Alpha and the Omega, the Beginning and the End, the First and the Last" (Revelation 22:13).

In addition, God created all things, including our concept of time. In some ways, it is unhelpful to ask what God did before the creation of the universe, since our concept of time was created as part of our universe. He exists outside of time and beyond time.

However, Scripture does hint at some aspects to consider regarding God's actions prior to our universe. For example, in John 17:24, Jesus said, "Father, I desire that they also whom You gave Me may be with Me where I am, that they may behold My glory which You have given Me; for You loved Me before the foundation of the world." God the Father and God the Son existed in perfect love, alongside the Holy Spirit, prior to the foundation of the world as part of the Triune Godhead.

Further, Ephesians 1:4 says, "He chose us in Him before the foundation of the world, that we should be holy and without blame before Him in love." In his amazing love and perfect plan, God chose those who would believe in him before creating our universe.

Matthew 25:34 also seems to indicate God planned eternity future prior to our universe: "Then the King will say to those on His right hand, 'Come, you blessed of My Father, inherit the kingdom prepared for you from the foundation of the world.'"

Another interesting insight is found in Titus 1:2, where Paul expresses his "hope of eternal life which God, who cannot lie, promised before time began." God prepared eternal life for us before time began. In other words, before the creation of our universe, a similar promise to the words of Jesus in Matthew 25.

Second Timothy 1:9 offers similar words about God calling us "according to His own purpose and grace which was given to us in Christ Jesus before time began." Our salvation was prepared for us before the beginning of our world. God's amazing love includes preparation countless years before our lives on this planet!

While salvation is by grace alone through faith alone in Christ alone, it is also a gift God has prepared far in advance. We should be humbled by his great love for us that includes not only our creation, but also the new creation of our hearts as we trust in him by faith.

In summary, God's known works before the creation of our universe include perfect fellowship within the Triune God, choosing those who would believe, planning eternity's future, and even preparing our individual time of salvation in Christ. While he certainly operated in other ways as well, these details found in Scripture offer strong insights into his power and love for us.

40. WHY DID GOD CREATE OUR WORLD?

While the Bible states emphatically that God created our world (Genesis 1:1), many wonder why he did so. Scripture offers several reasons to indicate his purposes for our planet.

First, God created our world for his own will. Colossians 1:16 makes this clear: "For by Him all things were created that are in heaven and that are on earth, visible and invisible, whether thrones or dominions or principalities or powers. All things were created through Him and for Him." God designed our world for his own desires and purposes.

Revelation 4:11 shares this conviction as well: "You are worthy, O Lord, to receive glory and honor and power; For You created all things, And by Your will they exist and were created." God's will or desire is major reason why our world exists today.

Second, God created our world to declare his glory. Psalm 19:1 rejoices, "The heavens declare the glory of God; And the firmament shows His handiwork." Isaiah 43:7 adds, "Everyone who is called by My name, Whom I have created for My glory; I have formed him, yes, I have made him." God's glory is the focus of his creative abilities.

Third, God created our world to demonstrate his wisdom. In Ephesians 3:9–10, the author describes the mysterious plan of God, "which from the beginning of the ages has been hidden in God who created all things through Jesus Christ; to the intent that now the manifold wisdom of God might be made known by the church to the principalities and powers in the heavenly places." It is interesting that this wisdom is revealed both to the church and to heavenly powers. The angels, demons, and even

Satan have seen God's creative wisdom on full display, revealing his greatness as above all other powers.

Fourth, God created our world in part to reveal his existence. In Romans 1:20 we find, "For since the creation of the world His invisible attributes are clearly seen, being understood by the things that are made, even His eternal power and Godhead, so that they are without excuse." His creative power reveals the Lord's invisible attributes, offering all people some degree of understanding regarding God's existence.

Fifth, God created our world to reflect his image. In Genesis 1:27, man and woman are created in his image. The image of God in humanity points toward the one who made us.

Sixth, God created our world to redeem it through the work of Jesus Christ on the cross. John 3:16 reminds us, "For God so loved the world that He gave His only begotten Son, that whoever believes in Him should not perish but have everlasting life."

These words also remind us of a seventh reason God created our world—to give his people everlasting life. He has a plan that involves creation and redemption. Both are part of his unfolding work that ultimately brings perfect glory to him.

41. CAN GOD BE KNOWN OUTSIDE THE CHURCH OR WITHOUT BEING PART OF A LOCAL CHURCH?

To answer this question, we must unambiguously define what it means to know God and define what a church is. When we talk about knowing God, we mean salvation by faith in Jesus

Christ (Ephesians 2:8–9). A person can clearly come to faith in whatever location or context God desires.

For example, Paul believed in Jesus after experiencing a vision on the road to Damascus in Acts 9. He was not part of a church, nor was he with a church congregation, but rather, he intended to arrest Christians. Salvation was in Christ alone.

Another example is found in the thief on the cross. He had no time to be baptized or join a church, yet he believed in Jesus by asking him to remember him when he came into his kingdom. Jesus answered his simple faith with the words, "Assuredly, I say to you, today you will be with Me in Paradise" (Luke 23:43). Jesus personally guaranteed the man's eternal life—beginning that day!

But what does it mean to be part of a church? The New Testament Greek word translated "church" is *ekklesia*, a word meaning "a gathering." We can believe in Jesus on our own, but we are not intended to live for Christ on our own. Outside of a local group of believers, there are many reasons why we cannot accomplish God's plans for our life.

For example, believers are to be baptized in obedience to the Great Commission (Matthew 28:18–20). Baptism requires other believers. In addition, Jesus calls his followers to practice communion, or the Lord's Supper, with other believers. Reading the verses concerning communion and taking bread and drink alone is not the same as participating in the Lord's supper with other Christians.

A look at the first church is helpful in this matter as well. Acts 2:42 teaches, "And they continued steadfastly in the apostles' doctrine and fellowship, in the breaking of bread, and in prayers." These early believers longed to meet together as much as possible. Their practices included learning, friendship, worship, communion, and praying together. Such community enhanced their faith in a way that was not possible alone.

A person can believe in Jesus outside of a local church, but trying to grow in faith outside of a local church is not an ideal situation. Church is essential to the maturity of a believer. Hebrews 10:25 teaches that Christians should not forsake "the assembling of ourselves together, as is the manner of some, but exhorting one another, and so much the more as you see the Day approaching."

We become a believer through Christ, not the church. The church is the community, but Christ is the Savior we follow. As believers, we treasure the church as the bride of Christ, but we find our salvation in Christ alone.

SECTION 5:

QUESTIONS ABOUT THE HOLY SPIRIT

42. WHAT IS SPEAKING IN TONGUES, AND HOW DOES IT APPLY TODAY?

Speaking in tongues is the spiritual ability to speak in another language. The first occurrence of this ability is recorded in Acts 2, where the first believers could speak in other languages so those visiting Jerusalem during Pentecost could understand the gospel message and believe.

Two other times in Acts, a group of new believers spoke in tongues as a group. This included those in the Roman centurion's home in Acts 10:46 and a group of about twelve men in Ephesus who were baptized in Acts 19:6. In both cases, the event appears to confirm God's Spirit at work in a new group of people coming to faith in Jesus.

Outside of the book of Acts, speaking in tongues is discussed as one of many spiritual gifts in 1 Corinthians 12–14. In this context, the ability is listed as a gift, with the note that not everyone would have this ability despite its importance.

In 1 Corinthians 13, two important points of discussion include verses 1 and 8. Verse 1 mentions "the tongues of men and of angels," a phrase some interpret as including a heavenly, angelic language. Verse 8 mentions a future time when speaking in tongues will cease. Some suggest this took place with the completion of the New Testament, while others believe this refers to Christ's return.

Even in the New Testament, there was much controversy regarding speaking in tongues. We should not be surprised to discover this issue often remains divisive today. However, the Bible is clear on some aspects of this ability.

First, speaking in tongues is not necessary to become a Christian. Some churches and leaders have wrongly taught that this ability is proof of knowing Christ. However, many examples are found in the New Testament of people believing without evidence of speaking in tongues. Further, salvation is by faith alone, not faith plus speaking in tongues.

Second, speaking in tongues appears to be a spiritual gift that not every Christian will have. First Corinthians 12–14 speaks on spiritual gifts in depth, indicating some believers will be gifted in some areas and not others. A Christian should never look down on a brother or sister in Christ because he or she does not speak in tongues.

Third, the area of speaking in tongues should be carefully evaluated within the church. For example, 1 Corinthians 14 states speaking in tongues (or languages) should be interpreted within church gatherings, yet many churches have completely ignored this teaching. In addition, church leaders and other believers should be respected regarding this issue, without seeking personal attention or divisiveness within a church.

Paul's conclusion of the matter in 1 Corinthians 14:39–40 remains important still today: "Therefore, brethren, desire earnestly to prophesy, and do not forbid to speak with tongues. Let all things be done decently and in order." Regardless of what a person or church believes on this issue, we are commanded to worship together in an orderly manner and to remember "the greatest of these is love" (1 Corinthians 13:13).

43. WHAT DOES IT MEAN TO GRIEVE THE HOLY SPIRIT?

Ephesians 4:30 says, "Do not grieve the Holy Spirit of God, by whom you were sealed for the day of redemption." What does it meant to grieve the Holy Spirit?

To grieve is simply to make sad. In the New Testament, grief is associated with lack of forgiveness toward others (Matthew 18:31). Jesus was also "grieved" at the hardness of hearts of certain people who opposed him (Mark 3:5). In 1 Peter 1:6, grief is contrasted with great rejoicing, indicating grief is the opposite of joy. The idea involves actions that would oppose God's will and his desires. How can a believer make the Spirit sad?

Scripture describes several ways earlier in Ephesians 4. For example, one way we can grieve the Spirit is to live like unbelievers (vv. 17–19). Specific actions listed in the verses that follow include lying, theft, unwholesome language, bitterness, and lack of forgiveness. Chapter 5 also addresses the ways sexual sins can grieve the Spirit.

In many of these areas, God provides both the problem and the solution. For example, instead of lying, we are to speak truth (4:25). Believers are not to steal but to work hard to meet the needs of others (4:28). We are to exhibit kindness (4:32), encouraging one another. Ephesians 5 begins by teaching believers to be "imitators of God."

A related teaching in the New Testament is the concept of quenching the Spirit (1 Thessalonians 5:19). Quenching includes the word picture of putting out a fire. When we sin, we dampen or lower the power of God's Spirit and impact in our lives.

The Bible often discusses our relationship with God as a loving Father caring for his child. As a perfect Father, he will not love us less when we sin or love us more when we do what is right. However, we can grieve or sadden God and his Spirit through our disobedience. When we place other priorities in our lives ahead of God or neglect time in his presence, it naturally saddens him just like a child disobeying or neglecting his or her dad.

Instead of grieving the Spirit, we are called to walk in the Spirit, remaining close each step of our lives with God's will for us. Galatians 5:16 specifically instructs us to, "Walk in the Spirit, and you shall not fulfill the lust of the flesh." Verse 25 adds, "If we live in the Spirit, let us also walk in the Spirit." Walking in the Spirit is an important part of our faith in Christ. When we walk in the Spirit, we experience closer fellowship and more effective service. We can accomplish far more when we walk in joy with the Spirit than we can live in our own strength.

Grieving God's Spirit does not change who God is, but it does change our ability to live for him. But when we walk by the Spirit and exhibit the fruit of the Spirit in our lives (Galatians 5:22–23), we bring joy to our heavenly Father and can better share the joy of our Lord with those around us.

44. WHAT DOES IT MEAN THAT THE HOLY SPIRIT INDWELLS A PERSON?

In 1 Corinthians 3:16, the apostle Paul asks believers the rhetorical question, "Do you not know that you are the temple of God and that the Spirit of God dwells in you?" God's Spirit indwells, or lives, in every believer, but what does this mean?

First, Scripture is clear the Holy Spirit indwells, or lives, inside every person when he or she believes in Jesus Christ. John 7:37–39 says, "On the last day, that great day of the feast, Jesus stood and cried out, saying, 'If anyone thirsts, let him come to Me and drink. He who believes in Me, as the Scripture has said, out of his heart will flow rivers of living water.' But this He spoke concerning the Spirit, whom those believing in Him would receive; for the Holy Spirit was not yet given, because Jesus was not yet glorified."

In addition, the Holy Spirit remains in believers for eternity. We don't lose the Holy Spirit because we disobey at some point along the way. He is always with us. Ephesians 1:13 says, "In Him you also trusted, after you heard the word of truth, the gospel of your salvation; in whom also, having believed, you were sealed with the Holy Spirit of promise." A seal protected and guaranteed the authenticity of a letter or document. In the same way, the Holy Spirit is a seal in your life as a believer that you belong to the Lord.

Third, because the Holy Spirit dwells within every believer from salvation throughout their lives, we can enjoy the power and presence of God's Spirit every moment. There is never a time when we are without God's Spirit.

This joyous truth should encourage us in many ways. We are never alone with God, as his Spirit lives within us. Further, we have strength to overcome temptation, as well as to face the problems of this life. Plus, we have the promise of 1 John 4:4 that "you are of God, little children, and have overcome them, because He who is in you is greater than he who is in the world."

The New Testament often builds upon the importance of God's Spirit indwelling within us. Especially powerful is 2 Corinthians 10:4–6: "For the weapons of our warfare are not carnal but mighty in God for pulling down strongholds, casting down arguments and every high thing that exalts itself against the knowledge of God, bringing every thought into captivity to the obedience of Christ, and being ready to punish all disobedience when your obedience is fulfilled."

The spiritual power within us as believers allows us to defeat the sinful thoughts and temptations we face. We will always face temptation in this life, but we will also always have power within us to help us defeat it.

The indwelling of the Holy Spirit is an important teaching of great value in the life of every believer. We must only recognize the Spirit within us and rely upon it in our daily walk with the Lord.

45. Why did the apostle Paul say the Holy Spirit is our deposit?

In the NIV, Ephesians 1:14 refers to the Holy Spirit as our deposit: "a deposit guaranteeing our inheritance until the redemption of those who are God's possession—to the praise of his glory." What does this mean?

The previous verse explains the Holy Spirit comes into our life at the moment we come to faith in Jesus Christ: "In Him you also trusted, after you heard the word of truth, the gospel of your salvation; in whom also, having believed, you were sealed with the Holy Spirit of promise" (v. 13 NKJV). This deposit is a way to guarantee our place in heaven with the Lord.

The Greek word is one that refers to marking with a seal. In New Testament times, a wax seal was placed on a letter or document to protect it and show the identity of the author. God's Spirit seals us in a similar way. We are protected by the Holy Spirit as well as identified as a child of God through this sealing.

This is one of the reasons we believe the Bible teaches that a true believer can never lose his or her salvation. If a person's faith is based on performance, we could certainly be at risk of turning against God or falling away. However, when we believe, God seals us, guaranteeing our future with him in heaven. We will make mistakes along the way, but make no mistake: God continues to hold us in his mighty hands.

Perhaps this is why Paul wrote in Romans 8:1, "There is therefore now no condemnation to those who are in Christ Jesus, who do not walk according to the flesh, but according to the Spirit." We walk according to God's Spirit now and are no longer under the control of the flesh or sinful nature in the same way as before we believed.

After a full chapter of building upon this hope, Paul concludes Romans 8:37–39 with these powerful words: "Yet in all these things we are more than conquerors through Him who loved us. For I am persuaded that neither death nor life, nor angels nor principalities nor powers, nor things present nor things to come, nor height nor depth, nor any other created thing, shall be able to separate us from the love of God which is in Christ Jesus our Lord."

Scripture is clear this deposit of the Holy Spirit is 100 percent secure. If neither death nor life nor any other created thing can separate us from the love of God, we can rest in his promise that we will spend eternity with him.

First John 5:13 agreed with these words when the apostle John wrote, "These things I have written to you who believe in the name of the Son of God, that you may know that you have eternal life, and that you may continue to believe in the name of the Son of God." God's Word doesn't say that you might have eternal life but "that you have eternal life." We can live with confidence in our future with the Lord, giving us boldness to better serve him today.

46. DID THE HOLY SPIRIT INDWELL PEOPLE IN THE SAME WAY IN THE OLD TESTAMENT AS IN THE NEW TESTAMENT?

The Holy Spirit clearly worked during Old Testament times (Genesis 1:2), but it did not operate in the same way as it does in believers since the time of Jesus coming to earth. In the Old Testament, the Spirit wrestled against evil people (Genesis 6:3), taught God's people (Nehemiah 9:20), and revealed God's presence (Psalm 51:11; 139:7).

In terms of working in the lives of individual people, God's Spirit empowered certain leaders but does not appear to indwell believers in the same way as today. For example, the Spirit came upon Saul but later left (1 Samuel 10:10). The Holy

Spirit later empowered David's leadership, but he feared losing this blessing of God's Spirit when he sinned (Psalm 51:11).

However, the Old Testament predicted a time when God's Spirit would work in the lives of all his people through the Messiah. For example, Isaiah 42:1 predicted, "Behold! My Servant whom I uphold, My Elect One in whom My soul delights! I have put My Spirit upon Him; He will bring forth justice to the Gentiles." Jesus the Messiah would be the one through whom the Spirit would work in a special way to all believers, including those who were not Jews.

Ezekiel 36:27 is another prediction of the Holy Spirit's future work in the lives of believers: "I will put My Spirit within you and cause you to walk in My statutes, and you will keep My judgments and do them." The Spirit would do more than work among God's people; it would be within them.

In the New Testament, John noted during the ministry of Jesus, "This He spoke concerning the Spirit, whom those believing in Him would receive; for the Holy Spirit was not yet given, because Jesus was not yet glorified" (John 7:39). It was in Acts 2 at the birth of the church that the Holy Spirit came in a way that began to indwell all believers.

In 1 Corinthians 6:19–20, Paul affirms the Holy Spirit's work in the life of every believer today: "Do you not know that your body is the temple of the Holy Spirit who is in you, whom you have from God, and you are not your own? For you were bought at a price; therefore glorify God in your body and in your spirit, which are God's."

The Holy Spirit doesn't only come upon certain people or at certain times anymore. Those who believe have God's Spirit within them at all times! This is why Jesus could say as he left this world, "I am with you always, even to the end of the age" (Matthew 28:20). Whether in prayer (Romans 8:26), living the fruit of the Spirit (Galatians 5:22–23), or other areas of living for God, we can know the Spirit is with us, helping us to live for the Lord. Jesus would not physically be with us always on earth, but the Holy Spirit lives within every believer, empowering us to withstand temptation, live with joy, and serve God's purposes in our lives today.

47. What is the difference between the Holy Spirit and the Spirit of Christ?

The Spirit of Christ is specifically noted in two verses of the Bible. In Romans 8:9, we see, "You are not in the flesh but in the Spirit, if indeed the Spirit of God dwells in you. Now if anyone does not have the Spirit of Christ, he is not His." The other verse is 1 Peter 1:11 that reveals, "the Spirit of Christ who was in them was indicating when He testified beforehand the sufferings of Christ and the glories that would follow."

In the verse from Romans, it is clear the Spirit of Christ is the same thing as the Holy Spirit and the Spirit of God. Father, Son, and Holy Spirit are the three persons of the one Triune God. Paul's emphasis was that knowing God required knowing his Son, Jesus Christ. Those who know Christ have his Spirit, the Spirit of God or the Holy Spirit, living within them.

In 1 Peter 1:11, the apostle referred to the prophets of the Old Testament. They spoke by the Holy Spirit, which was also the Spirit of Christ. In this way, Jesus was operating long before he walked on earth, as his Spirit empowered those who predicted his coming.

The concept of a Triune God who exists as one God in three persons is beyond our full comprehension, but it is not beyond our recognition. We see Father, Son, and Spirit as God, yet each having unique roles to fulfill in God's plan.

One exciting aspect of this study is that the Spirit who created our universe and raised Jesus from the dead is the same Spirit who works in our lives as believers! We need not fear any problem we face. Perhaps this is why Jesus said if we have faith as small as a mustard seed, we can move mountains (Matthew 17:20).

In addition to these two verses, Philippians 1:19 mentions the Spirit of Jesus Christ: "For I know that this will turn out for my deliverance through your prayer and the supply of the Spirit of Jesus Christ." In this context, the Holy Spirit is not immediately mentioned alongside the Spirit of Jesus Christ. These words could refer to the attitude of Jesus, but it is traditionally understood as parallel to the other verses above that equate the Spirit of Christ and the Holy Spirit. Others see the title as another name or designation of Jesus. In any case, the Holy Spirit is the Spirit of Christ working within us today.

Though Jesus is not with us today in human form, we know him through the Holy Spirit's power. One day, all of us who believe will see him face-to-face, experience not only his Spirit's work in our lives but also his very presence.

48. WHY IS THERE A HOLY SPIRIT IF THE FATHER AND SON ARE ALSO BOTH SPIRIT?

In early church history, a false teaching existed called Binitarianism. This belief held God consisted of Father and Son but did not include the Holy Spirit. In this view, the Spirit was simply another name for God the Father or the Son.

However, the Bible is clear that God is Triune, a view we also know as Trinitarianism. Father, Son, and Holy Spirit serve as the three persons of the Triune God. We see all three persons operating at once at the baptism of Jesus (Matthew 3:16–17), the Transfiguration (Matthew 17), and the Great Commission (Matthew 28:18–20).

Several other places in the New Testament make a clear distinction between Father, Son, and Spirit as well. For example, 1 Thessalonians 1:3–5 specifically refer to all three persons of the Trinity in the introduction, a format common to several of Paul's letters.

But why is there a Holy Spirit if Father and Son are also spirit? While a complete answer is not provided in Scripture, we can see some reasons for these differences. First, God the Father is unique from the Spirit in the sense that he operates outside of our universe as the Creator and sustainer of all things. In contrast, the Holy Spirit of God lives within every believer.

Second, Jesus came in human form to earth as part of God's plan. In contrast, the Holy Spirit came to indwell believers from the time of birth of the church (Acts 2). Jesus returned to the right hand of the Father and to dwell in the Father's house after his ministry on earth was completed. In contrast, the Holy

Spirit became involved in the lives of every believer through his ongoing presence to empower the followers of Jesus.

The Athanasian Creed sought to provide a written view to best reflect these aspects of the Triune God. Its words read in part:

That we worship one God in trinity and the trinity in unity,
neither blending their persons
nor dividing their essence.
For the person of the Father is a distinct person,
the person of the Son is another,
and that of the Holy Spirit still another.
But the divinity of the Father, Son, and Holy Spirit is one,
their glory equal, their majesty coeternal.
What quality the Father has, the Son has,
and the Holy Spirit has.
The Father is uncreated,
the Son is uncreated,
the Holy Spirit is uncreated.
The Father is immeasurable,
the Son is immeasurable,
the Holy Spirit is immeasurable.
The Father is eternal,
the Son is eternal,
the Holy Spirit is eternal.
And yet there are not three eternal beings;
there is but one eternal being.
So too there are not three uncreated or immeasurable beings;
there is but one uncreated and immeasurable being.

It appears part of God's unfolding plan includes a sequence of events that began by emphasizing the Father's role as Creator, the Messiah's role as Savior, and the Spirit's role as enabler. Despite these unique areas of operation, Father, Son, and Spirit have eternally existed as God and will forever exist as divine. We can appreciate the special work of the Holy Spirit in our lives today, knowing his work in us will come to full completion when we dwell with him in eternity.

SECTION 6:

QUESTIONS ABOUT WORLDVIEW

49. HOW IS FAITH CREDITED AS RIGHTEOUSNESS?

In Romans 4:3, we are told, "Abraham believed God, and it was accounted to him for righteousness." How is faith related to righteousness? How can it be a credit to us?

Throughout Romans 4, Paul gives examples to show how faith is credited as righteousness. His first example after Abraham is David. He declares in verse 7, "Blessed are those whose lawless deeds are forgiven, and whose sins are covered." Faith leads to forgiveness of sin. Because we are forgiven when we believe in Jesus, we are given his righteousness.

In the following chapter, we discover another reason faith gives us righteousness: escape from future wrath. Romans 5:9 teaches, "Much more then, having now been justified by His blood, we shall be saved from wrath through Him." Our faith keeps us from the punishment we deserve in judgment for our sins.

The end of Romans 5 offers yet another way faith is credited as righteousness—faith leads to eternal life: "as sin reigned in death, even so grace might reign through righteousness to eternal life through Jesus Christ our Lord" (Romans 5:21). We are given eternity in heaven with the Lord and his people through faith in Christ.

Romans 8 later describes the freedom we have in our faith with Christ. We have no condemnation, and nothing can separate us from him.

These four benefits—forgiveness, escape from judgment, eternal life, and freedom—offer wonderful "credits" of righteousness for our faith. Paul even identifies another relational benefit in Romans 4: we become a friend of God, just like Abraham was.

Before we believe in Jesus, we are considered enemies of God. Romans 5:10 explains, "If when we were enemies we were reconciled to God through the death of His Son, much more, having been reconciled, we shall be saved by His life." Colossians 1:21 adds, "And you, who once were alienated and enemies in your mind by wicked works, yet now He has reconciled."

As his children, we are no longer enemies but friends. Even better, we become sons and daughters of our heavenly Father, the one who loves us and prepares a place for us in the Father's house.

Romans 4:5 serves as the key to understanding how faith is credited as righteousness: "But to him who does not work but believes on Him who justifies the ungodly, his faith is accounted for righteousness." Our faith is not a work since righteousness is credited to "him who does not work." Instead, we believe on God.

Second, God is the one who justifies or makes us right with him. Nothing we do makes us righteous. It is what Jesus has done on the cross that makes us right with him.

Third, we are the ungodly Christ redeems. He was perfect, is perfect, and will forever be perfect. We were ungodly, stained by sin, yet he has given us salvation and new life. Through faith, God credits us with righteousness. We don't deserve it and cannot earn it, but we can glorify God for it and live with gratitude and love to him.

50. IS FAITH THE SAME AS A FEELING, OR IS IT RATIONAL?

Faith and feelings are related, but they are not the same thing. Faith involves belief and can be built on a combination of facts, feelings, and other influences, either right or wrong. In contrast, feelings are based on our emotions, are often changing, and are not always based on reality.

In the Bible, faith is defined in Hebrews 11:1 as "the substance of things hoped for, the evidence of things not seen." Notice it involves substance and evidence of the unseen. It includes what we do not see, but it is based on facts we can see and verify.

Hebrews 11 also includes what is often called the Hall of Faith or the Faith Hall of Fame, which lists numerous examples of people considered faithful throughout history. Examples include Abraham, Noah, Rahab, and David. Each was given a different level of evidence, yet these godly people placed their faith in the unseen God who could save them.

The evidence for the risen Jesus is a great example of faith versus feelings. The resurrection either happened or it did not, regardless of how we feel about it. Faith in the resurrected Jesus can be based on what we know about the facts of the event. We know Jesus died, he was buried, and his tomb was guarded. Yet on the third day, his tomb was empty, his body was never found, and many people claimed to have seen him alive again.

It takes faith to believe a dead man is alive again and is the Savior of the world. Our faith is a decision based on various facts. Feelings are closely associated with faith, but they change more frequently based on a variety of factors. Even our lack of sleep or food can change how we feel, but it should not change what we believe about God.

But does that mean faith is rational? It can be but is not always. Some people believe in UFOs, while others would consider this faith irrational. Some believe in gods made of wood or stone, but that doesn't mean their faith is rational or true. Yet rational thinking should lead to a consideration of faith rather than a rejection of faith. Critical thinking, properly understood, should strengthen our faith in God and his truth, as these convictions are based on facts rooted in historical events.

Faith regarding spiritual matters is not the only kind of faith. If you think about it, we have faith in gravity despite not completely understanding it. We have observed how gravity works, and we recognize the consequences of fighting against it. If we can observe and make conclusions regarding forces of nature such as gravity, why can't we make observations about the creator of gravity?

We don't believe whatever feels right. If we do, our faith rests on a shaky foundation that will not withstand scrutiny. Instead, our faith should be based on truth. Facts should lead toward a reasonable conclusion, including accepting that a supernatural God who created our universe can and did send his Son to defeat death and offer us eternal life.

51. WHAT ROLE DOES PHILOSOPHY HAVE IN THE CHRISTIAN FAITH?

Philosophy is known as the study of thinking. This field has often involved investigation of religious questions, such as the existence of God and of ethics. But what role does philosophy have in the Christian faith?

The first principle to consider is that we are to glorify God in all things, including philosophy. Colossians 3:17 teaches, "Whatever you do in word or deed, do all in the name of the Lord Jesus, giving thanks to God the Father through Him."

Second, we are called to know the reasons for the hope we have as believers. First Peter 3:15–16 declares, "Sanctify the Lord God in your hearts, and always be ready to give a defense to everyone who asks you a reason for the hope that is in you, with meekness and fear; having a good conscience, that when they defame you as evildoers, those who revile your good conduct in Christ may be ashamed."

Third, if our faith is true, we should not fear scrutiny from fields like philosophy. Philippians 4:8 reminds us, "Finally, brethren, whatever things are true, whatever things are noble, whatever things are just, whatever things are pure, whatever things are lovely, whatever things are of good report, if there is any virtue and if there is anything praiseworthy—meditate on these things." We are to think and consider what is true about our faith.

Fourth, understanding the views of philosophy can help us better share our faith with others. When the apostle Paul spoke with the Greek philosophers of Athens in Acts 17, he reasoned with them. While not everyone believed, some did, revealing the impact that knowing philosophy can have in reaching others with our faith.

Fifth, knowing philosophy can help us guard against wrong thinking. For example, Jude 1:3 says, "Beloved, while I was very diligent to write to you concerning our common salvation, I found it necessary to write to you exhorting you to contend earnestly for the faith which was once for all delivered to the saints." The idea of contending for the faith involves understanding the various views and perspectives to show what is right.

Despite these and other positive benefits to studying philosophy, there are some dangers to depending too much time and energy seeking human wisdom. Our power ultimately comes from God and his Spirit. When we rely on our own strength, there is a temptation to operate apart from the Lord's power and neglect his priority in our lives.

The apostle Paul warned of this danger in Colossians 2:8. It is the one verse that uses the word translated "philosophy," stating, "Beware lest anyone cheat you through philosophy and empty deceit, according to the tradition of men, according to the basic principles of the world, and not according to Christ."

We never need to fear philosophy as followers of Jesus, but we also recognize the limitations of human wisdom. While we strive to know all we can in our service for the Lord, we know he is the greatest source of power, far beyond the philosophies and wisdom of this world.

NEW TESTAMENT QUESTIONS

52. DID JESUS PREACH TO PEOPLE IN HELL?

Many people believe Jesus preached to those in hell after his death on the cross. The early Christian creed called the Apostles' Creed even states, "He descended into hell." Is this true?

The concept of Jesus descending into hell is from Ephesians 4:9–10: "(Now this, 'He ascended'—what does it mean but that He also first descended into the lower parts of the earth? He who descended is also the One who ascended far above all the heavens, that He might fill all things.)" This discussion refers to Psalm 68:18 in the Old Testament, referring to the lower regions or the earth. It is not a reference to Jesus going to hell but coming to earth.

In Psalm 16:10, some also suggest Jesus preached in hell because of the words, "For You will not leave my soul in Sheol, nor will You allow Your Holy One to see corruption." The term "Sheol" refers to the grave, though the King James Version translates it as "hell." It is easy to understand how people would believe Jesus descended to hell based on this older translation, but the term simply refers to the grave without reference to heaven or hell in this context.

Two other passages in the New Testament are also often mentioned to support the idea Jesus descended to hell. In Matthew 12:40, Jesus said, "For as Jonah was three days and three nights in the belly of the great fish, so will the Son of Man be three days and three nights in the heart of the earth." Some understand this "heart of the earth" as hell. However, the comparison with the "belly of the great fish" is the concept of death without a particular focus on hell or heaven.

The other passage used is 1 Peter 3:18–20: "For Christ also suffered once for sins, the just for the unjust, that He might bring us to God, being put to death in the flesh but made alive by the Spirit, by whom also He went and preached to the spirits in prison, who formerly were disobedient, when once the Divine longsuffering waited in the days of Noah, while the ark was being prepared, in which a few, that is, eight souls, were saved through water." Though difficult to understand, the emphasis appears to be on Christ announcing his victory over demons in the abyss rather than preaching to souls in hell.

The account of the thief on the cross helps us better understand where Jesus spent the three days between his death and resurrection. When the thief believed, Jesus said, "Assuredly, I say to you, today you will be with Me in Paradise" (Luke 23:43). Jesus did not go to hell. He left earth to return to his Father in heaven.

Because of these reasons, some denominations that use the Apostles' Creed in their worship services or in their hymnals even exclude this portion of the creed or include a footnote concerning this statement. The Bible is clear Jesus died and rose again. However, Scripture is also clear he did not go to hell. He returned to heaven with his Father (Luke 23:46).

53. WHO ARE THE ANGELS JUDE REFERS TO IN JUDE 1:6?

Jude 1:6 includes material many Bible readers find confusing. It reads, "And the angels who did not keep their proper domain, but left their own abode, He has reserved in everlasting chains under darkness for the judgment of the great day." Who are these angels?

The verse suggests that these are angels with problems. First, they "did not keep their proper domain." These words indicate they left their role as God's servants and their home in heaven, indicating these are fallen angels, also called demons or evil spirits in Scripture (Isaiah 14:12–21; Ezekiel 28:12–19).

Second, the Lord has these fallen angels in "everlasting chains under darkness." These fallen angels are currently under punishment for their rebellion against God.

Third, the reference to "the judgment of the great day" points to the final judgment of evil found after the millennial kingdom and rebellion in Revelation 20. Verses 11–15 describe the great white throne judgment and a lake of fire where those who have rebelled against God will be cast.

In addition to noting the identity of these beings as fallen angels or demons, many suggest these fallen angels are specifically connected with the sons of God in Genesis 6:1–4. Known as the Nephilim in Hebrew, these beings were so evil that they were part of the reason God chose to destroy the world with a global flood during Noah's time.

If so, these fallen angels appear to have been involved in creating families of people who were well-known during their time. Some suggest these were demon-human hybrids, with elaborate theories regarding human giants. However, it may simply indicate these Nephilim were influenced or possessed by evil spirits, leading to a culture of evil that experienced God's judgment. This would also help better explain the phrase in Genesis 6:4 that these kinds of people were also in existence after the flood.

Jude 1:6 also has a parallel passage in 2 Peter 2:4: "For if God did not spare the angels who sinned, but cast them down to hell and delivered them into chains of darkness, to be reserved for judgment." This verse occurs immediately before the mention of Noah and the flood. The same sequence is also found: angels sinned, they were removed from heaven, and they were placed in chains until future judgment.

Though outside of the Bible, the book of Enoch existed during New Testament times. It also mentions a Jewish tradition regarding some angels who sinned by having sexual relations with women. If Peter and Jude had this tradition in mind, it would provide further information beyond the Genesis account known to the readers.

Though uncertain, this is the most likely connection. Chronologically, this event did take place before the mention of Sodom and Gomorrah in Jude 1:7. Further, there is no other likely Old Testament reference to these activities, making Genesis 6:1–4 a reasonable interpretive decision.

54. Does Hebrews claim that Melchizedek was an early appearance of Jesus?

Melchizedek was a mysterious man noted in Genesis who is also mentioned in Psalms and Hebrews. In Genesis 14:18–20, we read, "Then Melchizedek king of Salem brought out bread and wine; he was the priest of God Most High. And he blessed him and said: 'Blessed be Abram of God Most High, possessor of heaven and earth; And blessed be God Most High, who has delivered your enemies into your hand.' And he gave him a tithe of all." We can observe he was a priest and king, known for serving the Lord. Melchizedek blessed Abram (later Abraham), with Abram giving him a tenth of what he obtained from winning a war.

In Psalm 110, David predicts the future Messiah's reign. Verse 4 proclaims, "You are a priest forever according to the order of Melchizedek." The Messiah would be a priest like Melchizedek, whose leadership is described as being without an ending.

The only other mention of Melchizedek is in Hebrews chapters 5–7. Hebrews 7:3 describes this priest as one "without father, without mother, without genealogy, having neither beginning of days nor end of life, but made like the Son of God, remains a priest continually." Just as David spoke of Melchizedek as a priest outside of the Levitical priesthood, the author of Hebrews confirms the many parallels between this priest and Jesus.

Both Melchizedek and Jesus were priests, kings, and without genealogy (in the sense that Jesus was born of a virgin), and the end of Melchizedek's life was not mentioned in Scripture. This has led some to conclude Melchizedek was an early appearance of Jesus (what theologians call a Christophany). However, this would only be true if these parallels are taken extremely literally.

The author's intent seems to focus on using the idea of Melchizedek to describe Jesus as a priest and king whose reign is without end. The author makes no clear comment regarding Melchizedek other than in relation to Jesus.

If taken literally, this would mean Jesus appeared as a human priest to Abraham to give him a blessing and to receive a gift of a tenth from him. However, it appears much more likely these aspects from the life of the human priest Melchizedek are used to illustrate aspects of the life of Jesus as the Messiah.

Hebrews 6:19–20 offers the best understanding of the relationship between Melchizedek and Jesus: "This hope we have as an anchor of the soul, both sure and steadfast, and which enters the Presence behind the veil, where the forerunner has entered for us, even Jesus, having become High Priest forever according to the order of Melchizedek." Our hope is in Jesus, the one who has become our eternal high priest. His priesthood is not like the Levites, who only served as high priest for a limited time, but rather an eternal priesthood, interceding on our behalf to God the Father.

The people of God no longer need a high priest to intercede behind the veil in the temple once a year on behalf of sins. Instead, Jesus our high priest offers forgiveness once and for all to every person who believes in him as Savior and Lord.

55. Did James teach a works-based salvation when he suggested faith without works is dead?

In James 2, the early church leader comments on the importance of believers who live out their faith through their actions. In 2:14–17, he strongly asserts, "What does it profit, my brethren, if someone says he has faith but does not have works? Can faith save him? If a brother or sister is naked and destitute of daily food, and one of you says to them, 'Depart in peace, be warmed and filled,' but you do not give them the things which are needed for the body, what does it profit? Thus also faith by itself, if it does not have works, is dead."

Does this mean we are saved by faith and works? Not exactly. Instead, James attacks the faulty argument that a person can be a true follower of Christ but not live for him. In the following verses, he argues that he shows his faith by his works (v. 18). He then follows with three strong examples to illustrate his argument.

First, he argues even demons believe there is one God, yet they are not saved. They believe and fear him, but they do not have an allegiance to him (James 2:19). Likewise, merely believing God exists and having a high view of him is insufficient. We must place our faith in him in a way that changes how we live.

Second, James refers to the example of Abraham. He states that Abraham believed in God, and he also obeyed God. Using the most extreme illustration possible, James reminds readers that Abraham was even willing to give the life of his own son to obey the Lord.

Third, James includes the example of Rahab. She was not a Jew but was a resident of Jericho and known as a prostitute. Despite her background, she showed her faith in Israel's God by protecting the Jewish spies (Joshua 2). God rescued her because her faith resulted in bold action to live for God. She even risked her own life to show what she believed.

James concludes in verse 26, "For as the body without the spirit is dead, so faith without works is dead also." If a person's life shows no change, James declares, the person is not truly a believer.

Salvation is by grace alone through faith alone in Christ alone (Ephesians 2:8–9). But the Bible is also clear salvation will lead to a changed life. You cannot become a follower of Jesus and stay the same. Jesus also said we could recognize people by their fruit. The fruit is not the source of salvation; it is proof of salvation.

In Matthew 7:15–20, Jesus explained a bad tree cannot bear good fruit and a good tree cannot bear bad fruit. A tree that does not bear good fruit is cut down and thrown into the fire, representing God's judgment. Verse 20 concludes, "Therefore by their fruits you will know them."

We don't need to doubt our salvation because our good deeds may not seem as big as the next person's. Instead, we simply live out our faith as an expression of belief in Jesus, revealing our faith by the good fruit in our lives.

56. Why did Satan want the body of Moses?

Jude 1:9 includes an event mentioned nowhere else in the Bible regarding the body of Moses: "Yet Michael the archangel, in contending with the devil, when he disputed about the body of Moses, dared not bring against him a reviling accusation, but said, 'The Lord rebuke you!'" What does this mean?

Many researchers have suggested this verse refers to an account in the now lost writing called the Assumption of Moses. The third-century church leader Origen noted this work and an account of Michael and Satan arguing over the body of Moses that closely relates to Jude 1:9. Whether Jude had in mind this writing or another oral or written account, this extra-biblical illustration was used to show that the false teachers of Jude's time were worse than the argument between the angel Michael and the devil!

Verse 10 adds, "But these speak evil of whatever they do not know." The false teachers were compared to Cain, who killed his own brother Abel; to Balaam, who prophesied for financial gain; and to Korah, who rebelled against the Lord and Moses. These examples highlighted the dire perspective of those who were compared to murderers, heretics, and lawbreakers.

In terms of the body of Moses, the Bible only says he went up to Mount Nebo across from Jericho where the Lord showed him the promised land. Deuteronomy 34:5–6, likely recorded by Joshua, says: "So Moses the servant of the LORD died there in the land of Moab, according to the word of the LORD. And He buried him in a valley in the land of Moab, opposite Beth Peor; but no one knows his grave to this day."

But why was there a conflict over his body? In one important study of the topic, early Jewish interpretations of Zechariah 3 were investigated in relation to Jude. These traditions suggest that

> the disagreement between Michael and the devil over Moses' body pertained not to the burial of Moses' corpse, as previous scholarship has assumed, but to Moses' bodily ascent into God's presence. In this ascent account, the devil would have opposed Michael on the grounds that Moses' fleshly, human body was inadequate for God's presence.[6]

It appears God had the final say regarding the body of Moses, burying him in an unknown grave. Does this mean the Assumption of Moses was an inspired book? Not necessarily. The New Testament writers quoted from a variety of sources without commenting on whether they were inspired. As in other forms of writing today, outside sources were sometimes helpful to illustrate teachings, using ideas familiar to one's readers.

For example, Paul quotes an unknown poet in Acts 17:28. Second Timothy 3:8 refers to an extra-biblical Jewish writing. Jude elsewhere refers to an event likely from the Book of Enoch. In Titus 1:12, Paul even referred to a prophet from Crete, stating, "One of them, a prophet of their own, said, 'Cretans are always liars, evil beasts, lazy gluttons.'"

In contrast, Jesus affirmed the Law, the Psalms, and the Prophets as inspired (Matthew 5:17–18). Paul noted Scripture was "God-breathed" (2 Timothy 3:16 NIV). The final chapter of the New Testament teaches that no one should add to or

---

6   Ryan E. Stokes, "Not over Moses' Dead Body: Jude 9, 22–24 and the Assumption of Moses in Their Early Jewish Context," Journal for the Study of the New Testament, vol. 40, no. 2 (December 2017): 192–213.

take away from Scripture: "For I testify to everyone who hears the words of the prophecy of this book: If anyone adds to these things, God will add to him the plagues that are written in this book; and if anyone takes away from the words of the book of this prophecy, God shall take away his part from the Book of Life, from the holy city, and from the things which are written in this book" (Revelation 22:18–19). The New Testament writers sometimes use outside sources, but they only refer to our Old Testament writings as the inspired words of God.

57. WHAT DOES IT MEAN THAT THE GOSPEL IS FOR THE JEW FIRST AND THEN FOR THE GENTILE?

In Romans 1:16, Paul wrote, "For I am not ashamed of the gospel of Christ, for it is the power of God to salvation for everyone who believes, for the Jew first and also for the Greek." What does it mean the gospel is for the "Jew first"?

The emphasis in this verse and in Paul's ministry appears to indicate that the gospel was sent to Jews first then to the gentiles. It was not a matter of importance but a matter of sequence. When Jesus first began his ministry, he first shared the gospel with Jews. This included the twelve disciples, who were all Jews, as well as the synagogues and other Jewish locations he visited. Though he sometimes shared his message with gentiles, he first shared with people from his own nation.

When Jesus prepared to return to the Father, he provided instructions to his followers. Acts 1:8 records, "You shall receive power when the Holy Spirit has come upon you; and you shall be witnesses to Me in Jerusalem, and in all Judea and Samaria, and to the end of the earth." Jesus sent his followers to reach all people, beginning with the Jews around them in Jerusalem.

However, it was not long before the gospel spread beyond the Jews. Following persecution, early believers took the message to others, including Philip taking the gospel to Samaria (Acts 8:4–8) and sharing Christ with a man from Ethiopia (Acts 8:26–40).

Peter soon also took the gospel to gentiles, beginning with Cornelius in response to a vision from the Lord in Acts 10. In Acts 11, Peter explains his missionary work to other church leaders, expanding the growth of the church to more people. Paul and Barnabas were ministering to Jews and gentiles in Antioch and were later called to their first missionary journey to gentiles across the Roman Empire (Acts 13:13).

Even during his missionary work, the apostle Paul generally spoke first in a city's Jewish synagogue. His strategy included reaching out to the Jews first, taking the message of the Messiah to his own people. When he was rejected in the synagogue, he would then minister to the gentiles in the city, often with tremendous results.

In Romans 1, the context is many years later, after Paul had shared the gospel in many locations but had yet to minister in Rome. Instead, he wrote to Roman Christians, encouraging them and looking forward to a time when he could teach among them. He would later spend two years in Rome under house arrest as described at the end of Acts 28, with further ministry that ended with 2 Timothy describing Paul in a Roman jail once again before his death.

The Jews were the people of the promise of the Messiah, but they were not the only recipients of the gospel message. Soon, the church would include more gentiles than Jews, making disciples of all nations just as Jesus commanded (Matthew 28:18–20).

Galatians 3:28 offers Paul's summary of the importance of both Jews and gentiles: "There is neither Jew nor Greek, there is neither slave nor free, there is neither male nor female; for you are all one in Christ Jesus." All people are equal. Our unity as Jews and gentiles is found in Christ, our Savior who makes us one.

58. Why did God strike Ananias and Sapphira dead?

In Acts 5, Luke shares an early account in the church where a married couple named Ananias and Sapphira are put to death by God. Why did the Lord abruptly end their lives?

Acts 4 ends with a summary that describes how some early believers sold their homes or land to donate to those in the early church, including Barnabas (Acts 4:34–37). In Acts 5, Ananias and Sapphira decided to sell "a possession," either a home or land, and they gave the money to the church as well. However, verse 2 explains that Ananias "kept back part of the proceeds, his wife also being aware of it, and brought a certain part and laid it at the apostles' feet." Instead of dedicating the entire amount, they secretly kept part of the money and pretended they had given all of it.

Peter confronted Ananias about this lie, and the man fell down dead. When his wife Sapphira later came before the apostle, her end was the same. But why did this occur? What were the reasons given for their deaths?

First, Peter said they had lied to God. Verse 4 shares, "You have not lied to men but to God."

Second, they tested the Spirit of the Lord. Verse 9 asks, "How is it that you have agreed together to test the Spirit of the Lord?"

Third, the event led to great reverence of the Lord Jesus. Verse 11 concludes, "So great fear came upon all the church and upon all who heard these things."

Though Ananias and Sapphira were likely believers, God still brought judgment upon them for their sinful action. Though less common in the New Testament, the Lord often judged people who disobeyed his commands in the Old Testament. This account served as a powerful reminder in the early church that the same God who judged the wrongs of his people in the past still held the power to do so in the church.

Some have also noted the seriousness of their sin may be associated with lying directly to the apostles, especially Peter. As those called to lead the early Christians, it was important for others to respect their leadership. Just as the Lord showed judgment upon those who rebelled against Moses, he likewise brought judgment upon those who rebelled against the leadership of Peter.

The words of Revelation 2:23 are also relevant on this issue. Jesus said, "All the churches shall know that I am He who searches the minds and hearts. And I will give to each one of you according to your works." The early church in Jerusalem was not alone in being judged for their works. Later churches were warned in this area as well. Still today, as individual believers and as congregations, we are called to obediently follow the Lord, or we may experience his judgment upon our actions. As

Jesus told the seven churches, "He who has an ear, let him hear what the Spirit says to the churches" (Revelation 2:29).

59. Does the Bible say it is an abomination for men to have long hair?

In 1 Corinthians 11:3–15, Paul addresses the issue of the hair length of men. Verse 14 includes the most direct statement, asking, "Does not even nature itself teach you that if a man has long hair, it is a dishonor to him?" Does this mean a man should not have long hair today?

Looking at only verse 14, it might appear this way. However, the context of the passage emphasizes the distinctions between men and women. The overall focus in this section includes men and women each serving within their unique roles, including an emphasis on how men and women are perceived as followers of Christ.

In addition, the law of Moses mentioned Nazirites, men who committed not to cut their hair for a certain time in devotion to God. Samson was a Nazarite from birth, and God commanded his family to never cut his hair. These examples reveal that men can at least sometimes have long hair and still be obedient in serving the Lord.

As Christians, Paul focuses instead on the concept that we are not to be ashamed of being created as a man or woman but should uncompromisingly identify as our God-given gender. Paul even included hair length as part of this identification. The goal is not a certain hair length but rather for men to look like and identify as men. In the ungodly society of Corinth, sexual immorality included a wide variety of issues, just as today. Paul wanted Christian men and women to look like men and women to not bring shame upon themselves or the church.

How far should we apply the application of this passage of Scripture today? Some suggest this teaching was limited to first-century culture and no longer matters. However, the general principle appears to remain important in our society. For example, we currently live in a nation where gender identity is a controversial issue. As Christians, we are called to accept God's creation of each person as male or female and live accordingly (Genesis 1:27–28).

In this sense, Paul's teaching can apply today by admonishing men not to seek to appear as if they were women. This may even have application to other related concerns, such as a man not dressing to look like a woman, a topic considered an important part of transgender culture.

However, how this is applied may vary. For example, the Nordic Vikings often had long hair, yet they would not have been considered trying to appear as female. Even many films of the life of Jesus portray Jesus and his disciples with longer hair, but they are still obviously male. Some men may even have a reason to have a certain hair length to minister to people in a certain culture, allowing opportunities for ministry rather than a focus on seeking to appear feminine.

Instead of focusing on a certain hair length as the issue, Scripture seems to emphasize our identity as men and women who follow Jesus. If we can at least agree on this application, our churches would be healthier than an environment that judges a Christian man for a certain hair length.

60. Should women still wear a head covering at church? Is it wrong for a man to wear a hat in church?

In 1 Corinthians 11, we find a discussion concerning women wearing head coverings during church services. Should women still wear a head covering in church today?

As strange as it may sound, some church traditions in America still follow this practice. You may see women wearing head coverings in some Pentecostal churches, among Anabaptists and Quakers, and it has a long tradition in many African American churches. There is even a modern "Head Covering Movement" that started in 2013 to bring back the long-lost tradition of women wearing head coverings. Though doing so is not wrong and is to be respected, a close look at the passage seems to show an emphasis on modesty and decency within congregational worship rather than simply covering one's head.

For example, still today in many Middle Eastern cultures, women commonly wear a headscarf in public. Not doing so is considered immodest and inappropriate. In first-century Corinth, this also seemed to be the norm among women in the city. However, when women came to faith in Christ, they learned about the freedom he gives, which led some to stop covering their heads.

While Paul often emphasized our freedom in the Lord, he also wanted women to continue with traditional modesty within church gatherings. He understood that a change in this area could appear improper and hurt the testimony of the church.

A similar tradition involves men not wearing a hat in church. In western culture, it has long been a sign of respect for men to remove their hats when inside, especially in a church building. Again, there is nothing wrong with this tradition, but to say the Bible commands men to never wear a hat in a church service is an application far beyond the intent of Paul's teachings.

We even see this regarding public prayers. Both of us have grown up in churches where men were told to take off their hats during a time of prayer. The tradition comes from 1 Corinthians 11:4 that reads, "Every man praying or prophesying, having his head covered, dishonors his head." As kids, we didn't know why, but we did it as a show of respect to those around us.

Instead of arguing over whether a woman should wear a head covering or a man should not wear a hat in church, our focus in gathering as believers is to worship the Lord and to encourage one another. As a church congregation, each church can help set appropriate guidelines to help accomplish this goal.

For example, in today's churches, those who speak or lead worship are sometimes asked not to display company logos. Why not? This can distract some members of the congregation from focusing on Christ to thinking about the brand of someone's computer, drink, or clothing, or it may advertise a company's ideas a church doesn't intend to communicate.

This could be a parallel to head covering or hat issues. Each church needs to consider how to best to address how people appear in their worship services, especially for church leaders, to keep the focus on worshiping God rather than other topics.

61. What does Paul mean when he says that women are saved through childbearing?

In 1 Timothy 2:15 we read, "Nevertheless she will be saved in childbearing if they continue in faith, love, and holiness, with self-control." Does this mean a woman is saved through having a child?

The answer is unmistakably no. Salvation is by grace alone through faith alone in Christ alone (Ephesians 2:8–9). There is no biblical example of a woman bearing a child and then being declared saved.

If it does not refer to salvation, then what does it mean? Some have wrongly suggested it indicates Christian women will be spared through childbirth. However, this cannot be possible, as many Christian women have not survived giving birth, nor is this idea found elsewhere ins Scripture.

Still a third inaccurate view suggests this verse refers not to childbirth but the birth of the Messiah descended from Eve. It is based on God's statement in Genesis 3:15 of the future Messiah: "I will put enmity Between you and the woman, And between your seed and her Seed; He shall bruise your head, And you shall bruise His heel." Though this is an accurate statement, it is not an accurate interpretation of the verse. A woman is not saved simply through Jesus being born of a woman but rather through faith in Jesus Christ.

Instead, the context appears to emphasize being saved in the sense of indicating perseverance. In other words, godly women will endure or make an impact through parenting children. This would best fit the immediate context in which Paul refers to Adam and Eve's role, their judgment, and implications for today. Verse 14 notes the woman was deceived but nevertheless remains vital through her role as the one who bears children in the marital relationship.

Genesis 3:20 affirms this concept as well. Immediately following God's judgment of Adam and Eve (as well as the serpent), we read, "Adam called his wife's name Eve, because she was the mother of all living." The next chapter records Eve giving birth to Cain and Abel, and later Seth, fulfilling the promise of God and the words of Adam.

While this interpretation makes the best sense of a difficult verse, how does it apply to women who are unable to bear children? This sensitive subject should be addressed carefully, but to be clear, this verse is about women in general rather than a specific woman. In the created order, women give birth to children, not men. We should not read into these words anything negative upon a person who has struggled with infertility or a miscarriage.

In addition, the verse emphasizes more than childbearing. The rest of verse mentions "if they continue in faith, love, and holiness, with self-control." Every Christian man and woman is called to these attributes. A godly woman will focus on faithful living, loving God and others, living holy before the Lord, and practicing self-control. These were teachings made in contrast to the sin of Adam and Eve when they lacked these qualities in the garden of Eden.

SECTION 8:

QUESTIONS ABOUT JESUS

62. DID JESUS REALLY CLAIM TO BE GOD?

Some critics argue that Jesus never claimed to be God. Is this true? A close look at the New Testament reveals that Jesus stated his deity in several ways.

For example, Jesus claimed to be equal with God the Father. In John 17:5 he said, "Now, O Father, glorify Me together with Yourself, with the glory which I had with You before the world was." Jesus said he was with God the Father before the creation of the world and shared his glory.

Second, Jesus also called himself the first and the last: "Do not be afraid; I am the First and the Last" (Revelation 1:17). He referred to himself as eternal, something only possible of God.

Third, Jesus called himself the "I AM," using one of God's names from the Old Testament. John 8:58 reads, "Jesus said to them, 'Most assuredly, I say to you, before Abraham was, I AM.'" The same God who revealed himself to Moses at the burning bush in Exodus 3 is Jesus.

Fourth, Jesus personally said he forgave the sins of others. In Mark 2:5, he said, "Son, your sins are forgiven you." Some of the scribes took offense at his words and responded, "Why does this Man speak blasphemies like this? Who can forgive sins but God alone?" (Mark 2:7). Jesus then answered their doubts with the words, "But that you may know that the Son of Man has power on earth to forgive sins" (Mark 2:10).

Fifth, Jesus claimed to be the Messiah. Many of the fulfilled predictions noted of him in the New Testament refer to messianic prophecies. Some of these include Jesus referred to as Lord in Matthew 22:43–44, quoting Psalm 110:1; his reference as the fulfillment as the Ancient of Days in Mark 14:61–64, alluding to Daniel 7:9; and his direct claim as Messiah in John 4:25–26: "The woman said to Him, 'I know that Messiah is coming' (who is called Christ). 'When He comes, He will tell us all things.' Jesus said to her, 'I who speak to you am He.'"

Sixth, Jesus accepted people worshiping him. Jews were taught not to worship anyone but God alone, yet Matthew 20:20 shows the mother of James and John bowing before him. The man healed from leprosy also bowed to him in Matthew 8:2, as did the healed demon-possessed man in Mark 5:6. The disciples also later prayed in the name of Jesus as God.

Seventh, the followers of Jesus called him God. In John 20:28, "Thomas answered and said to Him, 'My Lord and my God!'" In John 4:42, the woman at the well called him the Savior of the world. John 1:1 referred to Jesus as the Word who was God.

There are many other examples as well. The Bible consistently teaches Jesus claimed to be God in a variety of ways. It is clear his early followers referred to him as divine, as both the

Messiah and equal with God. Christians believe in the Triune God, consisting of Father, Son, and Holy Spirit as the three persons of the one Godhead.

63. ON WHAT DAY WAS JESUS CRUCIFIED?

Though Christians traditionally remember the death of Jesus on Good Friday, some have suggested other days, leading to doubt among people regarding which day is accurate. On what day was Jesus crucified?

The most direct biblical passage regarding the day Jesus died is found in Mark 15:42–43: "Now when evening had come, because it was the Preparation Day, that is, the day before the Sabbath, Joseph of Arimathea, a prominent council member, who was himself waiting for the kingdom of God, coming and taking courage, went in to Pilate and asked for the body of Jesus." The Sabbath was and is Saturday in the Jewish tradition, making Preparation Day Friday.

In addition, we can look at the date Jesus was resurrected. In Matthew 16:21 and Luke 9:22, Jesus predicted his resurrection on the third day. First Corinthians 15:4 affirms Jesus rose on the third day. All four Gospels directly state the tomb was empty on the first day of the week (Matthew 28:1; Mark 16:2; Luke 24:1; John 20:1). The first day of the week in the Jewish calendar is Sunday.

According to the Gospel accounts and early New Testament writings, Jesus died on Friday and rose on Sunday, calling it the third day. However, some argue this does not allow enough time for three days, since Jesus was only in the tomb parts of Friday and Sunday. Further, critics argue that this time frame does not fit his prediction in Matthew 12:40, which says, "As Jonah was three days and three nights in the belly of the great fish, so will the Son of Man be three days and three nights in the heart of the earth."

However, in the Jewish reckoning, a part of a day was often counted as a day. There was no concern in the early church regarding the count of Friday through Sunday as three days. A close look at the prediction related to Jonah is also helpful. Jesus did not claim he would be in the tomb for a full seventy-two hours. His comparison may have only focused on three days, which were marked by day and night (Genesis 1:17–18).

Those who argue for a different day for the crucifixion of Jesus do so in direct conflict with the biblical evidence. If the Scripture says he was on the cross and buried on Preparation Day (Friday) and the tomb was empty on the first day of the week (Sunday), why would anyone argue for another day of the week for these events?

Any other view must take a revisionist approach to the Jewish traditions of the days of the week. For example, a few interpreters have argued the Passover week included two Sabbaths, with a second one on Thursday with Jesus crucified on a Wednesday. However, this theory and others lack both biblical and historical evidence to support their views.

Instead of seeking an unjustified alternative, the straightforward reading of the New Testament shows that the crucifixion of Jesus on Friday. We call this Good Friday, as Jesus suffered in our place to pay for our sins through his death, ultimately defeating death through his resurrection on the third day.

64. Was Jesus or Paul the founder of Christianity?

While Jesus is traditionally credited as the founder of Christianity, some scholars have argued the apostle Paul was the one responsible for starting this new religion. Is there any truth to this view?

This view arose to prominence through a theologian named Gerd Lüdemann who argued that Paul and Jesus held views too different from one another and that the views of Paul became predominant in popularizing the Christian faith. However, a close look at the New Testament reveals that both Jesus and Paul shared identical views regarding essential Christian convictions.

Central to the Christian faith is Jesus as the resurrected Son of God. Jesus not only predicted his resurrection, but all four Gospels record the empty tomb on the third day (Matthew 28:1; Mark 16:2; Luke 24:1; John 20:1).

Paul would later write in 1 Corinthians 15:3–8 that he was sharing what had been revealed to him by the apostles: "I delivered to you first of all that which I also received: that Christ died for our sins according to the Scriptures, and that He was buried, and that He rose again the third day according to the Scriptures, and that He was seen by Cephas, then by the twelve. After that He was seen by over five hundred brethren at once, of whom the greater part remain to the present, but some have fallen asleep. After that He was seen by James, then by all the apostles. Then last of all He was seen by me also, as by one born out of due time."

His message was the same as the information Jesus gave his twelve apostles. This includes the death, burial, resurrection, and appearances of Jesus.

In addition to the resurrection, Jesus and Paul shared the same convictions regarding salvation. John 3:16 teaches, "God so loved the world that He gave His only begotten Son, that whoever believes in Him should not perish but have everlasting life." Similarly, Paul wrote in Ephesians 2:8–9, "By grace you have been saved through faith, and that not of yourselves; it is the gift of God, not of works, lest anyone should boast." Both emphasize salvation by faith or belief in Jesus as the only way of salvation.

Third, Jesus and Paul shared the same convictions regarding God's Word. Speaking of the Old Testament, Jesus noted, "For assuredly, I say to you, till heaven and earth pass away, one jot or one tittle will by no means pass from the law till all is fulfilled" (Matthew 5:18). Paul wrote, "All Scripture is given by inspiration of God" (2 Timothy 3:16). Both Jesus and Paul affirmed Scripture as from God, inspired, and unchanging.

While these and other similarities reveal the message of Jesus and the message of Paul were the same, there was a major difference. Jesus accepted worship as the Son of God; Paul worshiped Jesus as the Son of God. Paul did not invent Christianity; he developed the teachings of the faith as part of his calling in serving the Lord. God used Paul in a unique way to share the gospel and to pen many of the New Testament's books.

However, Paul himself declared, "I have fought the good fight, I have finished the race, I have kept the faith. Finally, there is laid up for me the crown of righteousness, which the Lord, the righteous Judge, will give to me on that Day, and not to me only but also to all who have loved His appearing" (2 Timothy 4:7–8). In the end, the apostle looked forward to being in heaven with his Lord Jesus Christ. Jesus was and is the founder of our faith and the author of our salvation (Hebrews 5:9; 12:2).

65. HOW DOES JESUS FULFILL THE MESSIANIC PROPHECIES?

The Old Testament lists several hundred prophecies regarding a future Jewish Messiah. Jesus fulfilled many of these at his first coming, with some still to be fulfilled at his second coming.

The earliest prophecy many connect with the future Messiah is found in Genesis 3:15. In God's curse on the serpent, we read, "I will put enmity Between you and the woman, And between your seed and her Seed; He shall bruise your head, And you shall bruise His heel." Satan would seek to destroy or attack the Messiah, but the Messiah would defeat Satan. Though vague in comparison with later predictions, this prophecy was fulfilled in Christ's defeat of Satan in overcoming death.

Of the more than three hundred messianic prophecies fulfilled in Jesus, many can fit in the categories of birth, ministry, and death and resurrection. The predictions of his birth become increasingly specific throughout biblical history. In Genesis 12:3, Abraham is promised all people on earth will be blessed through him. This specifically took place through Jesus, making a way for Jews and gentiles worldwide to experience salvation.

Later, God promised his covenant would be fulfilled through Isaac, with Jesus born through this family line (Genesis 17:19; Romans 9:7). He would come through Isaac's son Jacob

(Genesis 28:14; Luke 3:34) and the tribe of Judah (Genesis 49:10; Luke 3:33). He would come through David's family line (2 Samuel 7:12–13; Matthew 1:1), would be born of a virgin (Isaiah 7:14; Luke 1:35), and would be born in Bethlehem (Micah 5:2; Luke 2:4–7).

Many aspects of the ministry of Jesus were also predicted. First, he would be humbled in serving humanity (Psalm 8:5–6; Hebrews 2:5–9). He would preach to Israel (Psalm 40:9; Matthew 4:17), teach in parables (Psalm 78:1–2; Matthew 13:34–35), be rejected (Isaiah 6:9–10; Matthew 13:13–15), and would perform miracles (Isaiah 35:5–6; Matthew 11:2–6).

At the end of his life, Jesus would be a Passover Lamb (1 Corinthians 5:7) with none of his bones broken (Exodus 12:46). His blood would atone for sin (Matthew 26:28), he would suffer and die (Isaiah 53), and be resurrected (Job 19:23–27; John 5:24–29).

After his resurrection, Jesus predicted, "Nevertheless I tell you the truth. It is to your advantage that I go away; for if I do not go away, the Helper will not come to you; but if I depart, I will send Him to you" (John 16:7). This prediction was fulfilled as the Holy Spirit came at Pentecost in Acts 2 to start the church and begin empowering believers to spread the gospel.

Some of these predictions are amazing in detail. For example, approximately one thousand years before the crucifixion of Jesus, Psalm 22:18 predicted the clothing of the Messiah would be divided by casting lots, an ancient game of chance. In John 19:23–24, John describes how that took place exactly as predicted.

Imagine if we told you that in one thousand years, a certain person would be murdered and his clothing would be divided by a game of chance. The only way this could possibly come true would be through some type of supernatural information. The odds are so great as to be humanly impossible. Yet the Bible makes such predictions about Jesus as the Messiah over three hundred times, revealing the supernatural power of God's Word and the truth of Jesus as God's Son.

66. CAN WE BE SURE JESUS REALLY EXISTED?

People who dismiss the accuracy of the Bible may demand evidence outside of Scripture that Jesus existed. Otherwise, they argue, how can we know he even existed? How is Jesus different from other religious legends throughout history?

However, even looking at the Bible from a historical perspective, over five thousand New Testament manuscripts exist. These include many from within a century of the events. These manuscripts are higher in quantity and quality than any comparable ancient work. All twenty-seven books of the New Testament consistently speak of Jesus as a first-century Jewish man who claimed to be the Messiah.

In addition to the New Testament, many other early Christian documents exist that speak of Jesus. For example, the Didache is a Christian writing that provides a wealth of information about Jesus and his teachings from as early as the late first century. Some of the early church fathers, such as Clement of Alexandria, wrote within the first one hundred years of the birth of Christianity when some of the first-generation Christians still lived.

Outside of Christian writings, Jewish writings from the first century mention Jesus. The most well-known is the Jewish historian Josephus. In *Antiquities* he recorded, "James, the brother of Jesus, who was called Christ...who was condemned under Pontius Pilate to be put to death."[7] Elsewhere in the book, he shared, "At this time there was a wise man named Jesus. His conduct was good and He was known to be virtuous. Many people from among the Jews and other nations became His disciples. They reported that He had appeared to them three days after His crucifixion, and that He was alive; accordingly, He was perhaps the Messiah, concerning whom the prophets have recounted wonders."[8] Though not a Christian, Josephus offers early historical evidence of the existence of Jesus.

Greco-Roman writings in ancient times sometimes mentioned Jesus. Pliny the Younger noted early Christians believed Jesus was God. A second-century writer named Lucian recorded the crucifixion of Jesus, while Thallus mentioned a darkness that occurred at the time of the crucifixion.

Beyond writings, early historical events reveal at least some evidence of Jesus and early Christians. For example, in the mid-'60s, the fires of Rome were blamed on Christianity, leading to widespread persecution. This does not prove Jesus existed, but it does show a large group of Christians all the way in Rome willing to die for their faith just over thirty years after the crucifixion. It is highly unlikely these events would have happened unless a real man named Jesus actually lived in the time and place the New Testament records.

---

7   Josephus, *Antiquities of the Jews,* 20.9.1. https://en.wikisource.org/wiki/The_Antiquities_of_the_Jews/Book_XX#Chapter_9.

8   Josephus, *Antiquities*, 18.3.3.

Skeptics may like to claim there is no evidence to prove Jesus existed, but there is overwhelming information beyond the Bible to show he lived and did many of the works the Bible claims. We do not need to fear these attacks on our faith, but rather we should seek to show the reason for the hope within us (1 Peter 3:15–16).

67. HOW COULD ONE PERSON PAY FOR THE SINS OF EVERYONE?

Some people wonder how Jesus could pay for the sins of every person. However, Hebrews 10:12–14 is clear, "This Man, after He had offered one sacrifice for sins forever, sat down at the right hand of God, from that time waiting till His enemies are made His footstool. For by one offering He has perfected forever those who are being sanctified." While priests made repeated sacrifices for sins, Jesus paid one time for the sins of all people.

But how could the death of Jesus pay for all sins? The only way this was possible was because he was a perfect sacrifice. In 1 Peter 3:18 we read, "For Christ also suffered once for sins, the just for the unjust, that He might bring us to God, being put to death in the flesh but made alive by the Spirit." He suffered once because he is righteous and just.

Under the law of Moses, the Jewish people were required to regularly offer sacrifices for their sins. The priests at the temple provided daily offerings. Once each year, the high priest would enter the holy of holies to offer a sacrifice for the forgiveness of the people. These ongoing sacrifices were good but insufficient. Hebrews 10:1 states, "For the law, having a shadow of the good things to come, and not the very image of the things, can never with these same sacrifices, which they offer continually year by year, make those who approach perfect."

In 1 Peter 2:23–24 we read, "When He was reviled, did not revile in return; when He suffered, He did not threaten, but committed Himself to Him who judges righteously; who Himself bore our sins in His own body on the tree, that we, having died to sins, might live for righteousness—by whose stripes you were healed." Through his righteous sacrifice, we have been both forgiven and healed. He suffered in our place, allowing us to escape the punishment and judgment we deserve for our sins.

Does this mean all people are saved and will go to heaven? No, it does not. Jesus paid the penalty for every sin, but we must accept his gift of eternal life. John 1:12 says we must receive him to become his child: "As many as received Him, to them He gave the right to become children of God, to those who believe in His name." John 3:16 adds we must believe in Jesus as God's Son for eternal life: "God so loved the world that He gave His only begotten Son, that whoever believes in Him should not perish but have everlasting life."

When we do, we receive not only eternal life, but also abundant life. In John 10:10, Jesus tells us, "I have come that they may have life, and that they may have it more abundantly." Being freed and forgiven from our sins allows us to have a new life. This freedom gives us joy and allows us to bring the hope of Jesus to other people.

68. Who is the angel of the Lord in the Bible?

Many have debated the identity of the angel of the Lord. Some believe these appearances of the angel of the Lord are references to Jesus prior to his earthly birth, a view theologians call a "Christophany" or pre-incarnate appearance of Christ. This view emphasizes times when the angel of the Lord speaks as God, holds the responsibilities of God, or identifies himself as the Lord.

Several examples exist in the Old Testament. For example, in Genesis 16, the angel appearing to Hagar says in verse 10, "I will multiply your descendants exceedingly, so that they shall not be counted for multitude." Is this the angel speaking for God, or is it a physical appearance of God (also Genesis 21:17–18)?

In Genesis 22, Abraham prepares to sacrifice his son Isaac when he is stopped by an angel. In verse 12, the angel said, "Do not lay your hand on the lad, or do anything to him; for now I know that you fear God, since you have not withheld your son, your only son, from Me." Again, the angel is either speaking as God or is a human appearance of God.

Other Old Testament examples include Moses and the burning bush (Exodus 3:2), the angel of the Lord speaking to Israel in Judges 2:1–4 and 5:23, an appearance to Gideon in Judges 6:11–24, the angel of the Lord appearing to the parents of Samson (Judges 13:3–22), to David in 2 Samuel 24:16, and to Zechariah (1:12; 12:8). However, the angel of the Lord does not appear after the birth of Jesus in human form, leading to the conclusion by many that this angel revealed pre-incarnate appearances of Jesus.

However, not every Bible interpreter holds this view. For example, it can also be argued the angel of the Lord appeared to Joseph in a dream after Jesus was in the womb of Mary (Matthew 1:24). In addition, Scripture teaches, "No one has seen God at any time" (John 1:18; 1 John 4:12). If the angel of the Lord was an appearance of Jesus, it would appear to contradict these teachings.

But if the angel of the Lord was not the pre-incarnate Jesus, how do we explain the angel speaking and acting as God? He would have to be understood as speaking on God's behalf. In the ancient near east, this is how many messengers of a king functioned. The words of the messenger were spoken as if he were the king, with the full authority of the king. While it would be easier if these passages stated, "The angel said on behalf of the Lord," early readers could have easily understood the messages this way.

The major weakness of this view is that, in some cases, the person receiving the message believed they had seen God. For example, Hagar said, "Then she called the name of the LORD who spoke to her, You-Are-the-God-Who-Sees; for she said, 'Have I also here seen Him who sees me?'" (Genesis 16:13).

Because of the lack of clarity concerning the issue of the angel of the Lord, either view is possible. Also, in either case, this angel communicates a supernatural message of God that was important for the original recipient and remains valuable for us today. The accounts involving the angel of the Lord reveal God's love for people, his divine intervention in our lives, his supernatural power, and his unfolding will to redeem and save his people in times of need.

69. WHAT DOES IT MEAN THAT JESUS WAS FULLY MAN AND FULLY GOD?

The only way Jesus could be God is if he was 100 percent divine. The only way he could be human is if he was 100 percent man. But how could this view, known as the "hypostatic union," be possible?

First, let's look at how Scripture defines the humanity of Jesus. John 1:14 says, "The Word became flesh and dwelt among us, and we beheld His glory, the glory as of the only begotten of the Father, full of grace and truth." Jesus was eternally divine in the past, yet he took on humanity, or "became flesh," to live on the earth. In 1 John 4:2 we read, "By this you know the Spirit of God: Every spirit that confesses that Jesus Christ has come in the flesh is of God." Jesus "came in the flesh" through his virgin birth in Mary's womb.

Second, let's consider what the Bible says about the divine nature of Jesus. John 1:1–3 says, "In the beginning was the Word, and the Word was with God, and the Word was God. He was in the beginning with God. All things were made through Him, and without Him nothing was made that was made." Jesus is eternal, is God, and all things were made through him. He did not stop being God to become human though he chose not to use all his divine powers during his earthly life.

Third, let's consider how these two natures are united as one. Hebrews 1:2–3 says, "In these last days [God has] spoken to us by His Son, whom He has appointed heir of all things, through whom also He made the worlds; who being the brightness of His glory and the express image of His person, and upholding all things by the word of His power, when He had by Himself purged our sins, sat down at the right hand of the Majesty on high." God's image was in the person of Jesus, providing a way to God through his forgiveness of our sins.

Jesus also spoke of himself as one person. He was equal with God the Father and God the Spirit, yet he existed as God the Son. John 17:23 says, "I in them, and You in Me; that they may be made perfect in one, and that the world may know that You have sent Me, and have loved them as You have loved Me."

This divine and human nature allowed Jesus to identify with us as humans, yet without sinning. Hebrews 4:15–16 teaches, "We do not have a High Priest who cannot sympathize with our weaknesses, but was in all points tempted as we are, yet without sin. Let us therefore come boldly to the throne of grace, that we may obtain mercy and find grace to help in time of need." The application for us today should not be confusion but rather boldness to approach God's throne of grace with our needs.

The humanity and deity of Jesus are both essential to his role as the Son of God. He has identified with the human experience while also creating all humanity. This great power and love reveal his care for us and should lead us to a deeper worship of our Lord.

70. WHAT HAPPENED TO JESUS BETWEEN HIS BIRTH AND HIS EARTHLY MINISTRY?

The birth of Jesus is recorded twice, in both Matthew 1–2 and Luke 1–2. However, we are told little of what happened to him between his birth and his earthly ministry at around the age of thirty years old. What happened during this time?

Both Matthew and Luke give some details about the life of Jesus after his birth. More is actually told than we often realize:

- He was visited by shepherds on the night of his birth (Luke 2:8–20).

- On the eighth day, Jesus was circumcised and officially given his name according to Jewish tradition (Luke 2:21).

- Joseph and Mary took Jesus to Jerusalem about forty days after his birth for purification rites where they met Simeon and Anna (Luke 2:25–38).

- Wise men visited the family in a house, either before or after this visit to Jerusalem (Matthew 2:1–12).

- Joseph, Mary, and Jesus fled to Egypt from Bethlehem to escape death, living there until after Herod's death in approximately 4 BC (Matthew 2:13–14).

- Joseph, Mary, and Jesus moved back to their hometown of Nazareth (Matthew 2:22–23).

- Joseph and Mary had additional children, including sons James, Joseph, Judas, and Simon, and at least two daughters (Matthew 13:55–56; Mark 6:3).

- Jesus visited Jerusalem with his family at the age of twelve and remained in the temple three days while his parents searched for him (Luke 2:41–48).

- Jesus "increased in wisdom and stature, and in favor with God and men" (Luke 2:52).

-He also likely learned carpentry under his father Joseph during this time and was known as "the carpenter's son" until his ministry (Matthew 13:55).

-His relative John the Baptist preached and baptized, preparing the way for the ministry of Jesus. Jesus was baptized by John at the start of his ministry. John's ministry may have taken place when Jesus was in his twenties, meaning the Gospels only leave the period between the ages of twelve to his mid-twenties silent regarding the early life of Jesus.

The Bible does not mention his father Joseph during Jesus' earthly ministry, indicating that Joseph likely died sometime between the time Jesus was twelve and thirty years old. Perhaps Jesus was responsible for helping lead his mother and siblings until his younger siblings were old enough to do so.

The Gospel of Thomas, a second-century writing not authored by the apostle Thomas, recounts stories from the so-called lost years of Jesus. This writing, though likely fictional, showed that even at this early time, there was interest in the childhood years of Jesus.

Because the focus in the four Gospels was on the ministry of Jesus, including his teachings, miracles, and death and resurrection, they mostly write concerning the time his ministry began. This period covered a little over three years and included much activity.

We should be thankful for how much information is preserved about the early life of Jesus and emphasize what the Bible highlights—his ministry, death, and resurrection. Jesus came to bring us new life, a message we need to share with others today.

71. HOW COULD MARY GIVE BIRTH TO JESUS AS A VIRGIN?

Human history notes the birth of Jesus as unique in many ways, but the virgin birth certainly stands out as the most significant. How could Mary give birth as a virgin?

The Bible explains this act in two ways—as a miracle and as a fulfillment of prophecy. First, a woman giving birth without sexual contact is considered impossible but not to God. When the angel told Mary she would have a child even though she was still a virgin, she asked how this would be possible. The angel answered, "With God nothing will be impossible" (Luke 1:37). The One who made the laws that govern our universe—and our bodies—can intervene as he chooses.

Second, the Bible explains the virgin birth as a fulfillment of Bible prophecy. In Matthew 1:22–23, Matthew quotes from Isaiah 7:14, writing, "So all this was done that it might be fulfilled which was spoken by the Lord through the prophet, saying: 'Behold, the virgin shall be with child, and bear a Son, and they shall call His name Immanuel,' which is translated, 'God with us.'"

Modern science has sometimes attempted to speculate, offering various medical theories to help explain how a virgin could give birth. While some theories have been suggested, there is no clear human answer to provide a non-miraculous explanation for a virgin birth. Instead, even if a method could be provided, only God's perfect timing in the life of Mary would have made her virgin birth possible in fulfilment of Bible prophecy.

In fact, in addition to the virgin birth, numerous other prophecies were fulfilled at the birth of Christ that point to God's supernatural power as the only source. For example, the Messiah would be born in Bethlehem, the town of David (Micah 5:2). Mary lived in Nazareth, yet she was forced to travel to Bethlehem for a census. Talk about God's timing! Otherwise, this prophecy would not have been accurately fulfilled.

Further, Jesus had to be descended from Abraham and born of the tribe of Jacob and the family of David (Jeremiah 23:5–6). After his birth, he would be called out of Egypt, a prophecy fulfilled when Jesus and his family fled to Egypt to avoid death from Herod soldiers (Hosea 11:1; Matthew 2:1–15).

Even this event was predicted in Scripture, as Jeremiah 31:15 prophesied, "A voice was heard in Ramah, Lamentation and bitter weeping, Rachel weeping for her children, refusing to be comforted for her children, because they are no more." Matthew 2:17–18 shows that this as an exact fulfillment of a prediction made more than six hundred years earlier. Jesus would even be called a Nazarene, a prediction noted by Matthew 2:23 that was fulfilled by Jesus and his family returning to Nazareth when he was young.

Just as the virgin birth of Jesus was a miracle, God confirmed Jesus as the Messiah through multiple prophecies centuries in advance. These predictions were fulfilled with such amazing accuracy that those who review them can hardly point to chance but rather to the power of God.

SECTION 9:

QUESTIONS ABOUT SALVATION

72. WHAT IS THE UNPARDONABLE SIN, AND CAN WE COMMIT IT TODAY?

Matthew 12:31–32 mentions a sin God will not forgive: "Therefore I say to you, every sin and blasphemy will be forgiven men, but the blasphemy against the Spirit will not be forgiven men. Anyone who speaks a word against the Son of Man, it will be forgiven him; but whoever speaks against the Holy Spirit, it will not be forgiven him, either in this age or in the age to come." What is this unforgivable or unpardonable sin? Can we commit it today?

The text states the sin is "blasphemy against the Spirit." However, many wonder what this means. The context of Matthew 12 reveals that those who saw the miracles Jesus had performed were attributing his power to Satan. Instead of accepting the Spirit's work as being from God, they accused it of being from the devil. This was the unforgivable sin. These religious teachers would not be forgiven of calling God's works the works of Satan.

But does this mean we can commit the unpardonable sin today? Not exactly. Like those who watched Jesus perform miracles, a person can still choose to attribute the power of God as being from the devil and die as an unbeliever apart from God. But unlike when Jesus spoke these words, we are not forever condemned if we make such a statement in a time of weakness. Jesus condemned a specific group of people for a specific act against the Lord. Therefore, it appears this unpardonable sin is unable to be committed in the same way today.

The larger question is whether our sin will keep us from heaven or not. Jesus taught we receive eternal life through faith in him (John 3:16). There is no other name under heaven by which we must be saved (Acts 4:12). There is also no good deed or work we can do that is sufficient to forgive our own sins and provide eternal life (Ephesians 2:8–9). The only way to escape the judgment of sin is through faith in Jesus Christ.

Those who truly believe in him do not need to fear somehow losing this gift. Nothing can separate us from the love of God (Romans 8:37–39). Instead, we praise God for the gift of eternal life. We seek to be transformed by the renewing of our minds (Romans 12:1–2). We are called to mature in our faith, to show God's love, and to share Christ with others, making disciples of all nations (Matthew 28:18–20).

Even as believers, we still often commit sins. When we do, we are called to confess them. First John 1:9 teaches, "If we confess our sins, He is faithful and just to forgive us our sins and to cleanse us from all unrighteousness." We do not need to be saved every day and receive a daily conversion, but we do need daily confession. This pattern of confessing our sins before the Lord allows us to remain in close fellowship with him and effectively fulfill his call for our lives.

However, we can take great comfort in knowing there is nothing we can do to make God love us any more or any less. Our heavenly Father loves us perfectly, just as we are. He wants to help us grow and help others as we seek to avoid sin and pursue his plans for our future.

73. Does Hebrews 6 indicate that we can lose our salvation?

Those who believe a Christian can lose his or her salvation often base this belief on Hebrews 6:4–6: "For it is impossible for those who were once enlightened, and have tasted the heavenly gift, and have become partakers of the Holy Spirit, and have tasted the good word of God and the powers of the age to come, if they fall away, to renew them again to repentance, since they crucify again for themselves the Son of God, and put Him to an open shame." How are we to understand these verses?

The key phrase to understand is "those who were once enlightened." Were these people who were saved? If so, then it seems they include people who can lose their salvation. However, it appears this is not the case. Those who were once enlightened are those familiar with the gospel but who have never genuinely accepted it. Because they knew the truth and refused it, there was nothing else to be done for them. They would die apart from Christ despite knowing exactly how to live with him for eternity.

These unbelievers were given a variety of opportunities. In addition to being enlightened, they "had tasted the heavenly gift." This means they had a sample of what it means to know Christ from being around other followers of Christ. This may have included people who attended worship services and saw how God had changed the lives of others but who had never believed for themselves.

Third, they were called "partakers of the Holy Spirit." To partake means to participate. They had seen the Holy Spirit work around them but had still not converted to faith in Jesus. A good example of this is found in Acts 2. Even though three thousand believed in Jesus that day (Acts 2:41), others were not convinced and accused the disciples of being drunk. They saw the Spirit's power, yet they refused to believe.

Fourth, these unbelievers had "tasted the good word of God." They had heard Scripture, likely the Old Testament books of the Bible, yet refused to believe. Unlike many in that time and still today who have never heard the Word of God, these individuals had access to Scripture but did not believe it.

Fifth, these unbelievers tasted in "the powers of the age to come." This phrase is less certain regarding its meaning. It may allude to the role of angels and the role of spiritual warfare in the church. Ephesians 6:10–18 certainly emphasizes this area as an important part of the Christian life. If so, these unbelievers witnessed God's work during spiritual battles and yet were not saved.

These verses note that when a person experiences these activities and still falls away, there is no other hope. The words compare their actions to crucifying Jesus all over again, something it calls an "open shame" or public shame.

In our churches today, there are many people who have read the Bible, seen God work, and have heard the gospel, yet have never personally believed. If we refuse to believe despite these clear examples of God at work around us, Scripture is clear that we will be judged. If you fall in this category, we urge you to trust in Christ before it is too late. You have seen God's hand at work. Believe in Jesus to save you so you can experience eternal life.

74. WILL I KNOW MY LOVED ONES IN HEAVEN?

In addition to being in heaven for eternity with the Lord as believers, we will enjoy eternity with every other believer. But many have asked whether we will be able to recognize or know our loved ones in the afterlife. What does the Bible teach about recognizing loved ones in heaven?

The Bible may not give as many details as we would like on this topic, but we can observe some aspects about this part of heaven. For example, when David's infant son died, he said, "Now he is dead; why should I fast? Can I bring him back again? I shall go to him, but he shall not return to me" (2 Samuel 12:23). David fully expected to see his son—and recognize him—in heaven.

A second example is found in the account of Lazarus and the rich man in Luke 16. Both Abraham and Lazarus are able to see one another in heaven. Interestingly, they can also identify the rich man who is in hell.

A third example is found at the Transfiguration of Jesus. Peter, James, John, and Jesus saw Moses and Elijah after their deaths in glorified bodies and could clearly recognize them (Matthew 17:3–4).

Before Jesus was crucified, he shared the Last Supper with his followers. During this meal, he promised that he would share a meal with them again in the kingdom of God (Matthew 8:11; Luke 22:17–18). If the disciples will recognize Jesus and one another in heaven, it seems likely to conclude we will know one another in heaven as well.

Many have also noted that others could identify the resurrected body of Jesus. Though his identity was hidden for a time from the two disciples during a walk to Emmaus (Luke 24:13–35), Jesus was almost always clearly identified, including the scars on his feet and hands (John 20:27–28).

In a general sense, 1 Corinthians 13:12 talks about a future time when we will "know fully" (NIV). It is clear that we will know more in heaven, not less. This verse also supports the conviction that we will clearly know the identities of our loved ones in heaven.

We can also find comfort in the many faithful followers of God listed in Hebrews 11. People like Abraham, Moses, David, and Rahab are listed as people "of whom the world was not worthy" (Hebrews 11:38). Yet today they are in heaven, with identities certainly known to God and to others.

Those who believe in Christ today can likewise take comfort in the hope that we will know our loved ones who are in heaven. Even 1 Thessalonians 4:17–18 speaks of Jesus taking believers to heaven in the future with the teaching to comfort one another with these words. We anticipate heaven as a wonderful future where we will rejoice with our believing loved ones for all eternity as we worship the Lord.

75. ARE THE PEOPLE WHO GO TO HEAVEN NOW ANGELS?

Some people have been taught that those who go to heaven become angels and "earn their wings." Maybe you've even heard someone say, "Heaven gained another angel," when a loved one has died. Does the Bible support the belief that people become angels in heaven?

A biblical look at angels reveals all angels who will ever exist have already been created. People do not turn into angels in heaven. Let's first look at what the Bible teaches about the soul of a person upon death. A person who does not know Christ will be eternally separated from God (Matthew 25:46). In contrast, those who believe in Jesus will enjoy eternity with the Lord (Philippians 1:23).

But what will a person look like or be like in heaven? We are given some hints but not as much information as we would like. For example, at the Transfiguration (Matthew 17), Moses and Elijah appeared with Jesus. Peter, James, and John witnessed the event and recognized them as people, not as angels.

The New Testament also teaches that every believer will one day receive a new, glorified body. First Corinthians 15:52–53 describes, "The trumpet will sound, and the dead will be raised incorruptible, and we shall be changed. For this corruptible must put on incorruption, and this mortal must put on immortality."

Even the resurrected Jesus gives us some insight into our heavenly bodies. When he appeared to his followers, they clearly recognized him as Jesus. His body was resurrected, but he maintained his personal physical traits.

But what about angels? They were created by God (Colossians 1:16–17) to serve the Lord (Luke 2:13) and minister to people (Acts 8:26). From the description in Colossians 1:16–17, it appears all angels were created at the same time. They were certainly created within the first six days of creation (Exodus 20:11).

In some cases, angels appeared in human form (Daniel 8:15), but at other times, the Bible clearly describes them as angelic beings (Ezekiel 1:5–11). Psalm 148:5 includes angels in the list of items God created, exclaiming, "Let them praise the name of the Lord, For He commanded and they were created."

The Bible describes at least three types of angels. They include cherubim (Genesis 3:24; Ezekiel 10:1–22), seraphim (Isaiah 6:2–7), and living creatures (Ezekiel 1:5–14; Revelation 4:6–8). They also include some type of ranking, with Michael noted as an archangel in Jude 1:9. First Thessalonians 4:16 suggests there may be other archangels as well. Gabriel was specifically noted as an angel by name, bringing the message to Mary concerning the virgin birth of Jesus (Luke 1).

Instead of humans turning into angels in heaven, believers will worship the Lord in heaven. Revelation describes a time when every being in the heavenlies will bow before the Lord: "Blessing and honor and glory and power Be to Him who sits on the throne, And to the Lamb, forever and ever!" (Revelation 5:13).

76. WHAT DOES IT MEAN FOR A CHRISTIAN TO BACKSLIDE?

Churches have long used the term "backsliding" to refer to a Christian who stops growing and living in obedience to the Lord. While the Bible does not use the same wording, it certainly challenges believers to live completely devoted to God rather than being mediocre.

In Revelation 3:15–16, Jesus commanded the Christians in Laodicea to stop being lukewarm (neither cold nor hot) and live totally for God: "I know your works, that you are neither cold nor hot. I could wish you were cold or hot. So then, because you are lukewarm, and neither cold nor hot, I will vomit you out of My mouth."

Further, believers are called to follow the Great Commandment that teaches: "You shall love the LORD your God with all your heart, with all your soul, and with all your mind" (Matthew 22:37). A follower of Jesus is challenged to serve with 100 percent commitment.

Despite the Bible's commands to love God with all our heart, soul, and mind, we don't lose our faith or salvation when we sin. Nothing can separate us from God's love (Romans 8:37–39). When we disobey, we may experience some judgment in this life or lose spiritual rewards in heaven, but we do not lose our salvation.

Instead, when we sin, we are called to confess our sins and receive God's forgiveness: "If we confess our sins, He is faithful and just to forgive us our sins and to cleanse us from all unrighteousness" (1 John 1:9). God desires close fellowship with us and that we live a life free from ongoing sin and rebellion.

Even the strongest followers of Jesus sin at times. For example, on the night Jesus was betrayed, he was not only given over to the authorities by Judas Iscariot, but he was also abandoned by all his followers. Peter denied three times that he even knew Jesus. Yet Peter was soon restored to ministry (John 21) while all the disciples except Judas returned to live for Jesus until their deaths.

Jesus calls us to not to grow weary in doing good (Galatians 6:9). In addition, we are to do all we can to help other believers who are weak or have turned from the Lord. James 5:19–20 teaches, "Brethren, if anyone among you wanders from the truth, and someone turns him back, let him know that he who turns a sinner from the error of his way will save a soul from death and cover a multitude of sins."

Luke 15 offers a picture of God's attitude toward believers who backslide. The story of the prodigal son describes how the father remained faithful despite the wayward actions of his son. The son wasted his gifts and ended up in worse condition than the father's servants. The son then returned to his father, uncertain of what to expect.

Luke 15:20 teaches, "When he was still a great way off, his father saw him and had compassion, and ran and fell on his neck and kissed him." The father was waiting for his return, had compassion on him when he returned, and embraced him with love. This is the attitude of our heavenly Father. No matter what we have done, he will embrace us if we return to him.

77. How will I be able to enjoy heaven if I know there are people in hell?

Revelation 21–22 describe a new heaven and earth where all God's people will live in perfect joy with him for all eternity. Revelation 21:4 specifically teaches, "God will wipe away every tear from their eyes; there shall be no more death, nor sorrow, nor crying. There shall be no more pain, for the former things have passed away." But how can we be happy if we have loved ones and know many other people who will be in hell?

From our human perspective, it does not make sense that we can experience perfect joy while knowing others are suffering. However, there are some concepts to help. First, when we are in heaven, we will see things from God's perspective. God is love and judges perfectly. When we see reality from his point of view, we will be equipped to handle the concepts that are impossible for us to currently understand from our limited earthly perspective.

First Corinthians 13:12 teaches, "For now we see in a mirror, dimly, but then face to face. Now I know in part, but then I shall know just as I also am known." Paul knew there would be a day when we would better understand reality as God does. We may not understand how we can rejoice while others are eternally separated from God, but we will when we are with the Lord and know fully.

We must also continue to remember God's patience. He does not send people to hell because he desires to punish people. God wants all people to repent and turn to him. Second Peter 3:8–9 teaches, "But, beloved, do not forget this one thing, that with the Lord one day is as a thousand years, and a thousand years as one day. The Lord is not slack concerning His promise, as some count slackness, but is longsuffering toward us, not willing that any should perish but that all should come to repentance."

In heaven, God will change our perspective regarding those in heaven and hell. We will both enjoy his presence and will understand his judgment upon those apart from him.

In Revelation 6:10, we see some in heaven who already call upon God's judgment of the wicked: "How long, O Lord, holy and true, until You judge and avenge our blood on those who dwell on the earth?" They were with the Lord, yet they asked God to judge those who are evil, all as part of the Lord's divine plan.

After God judges the wicked in the future, people will rejoice. Why? They will understand this judgment is part of God's plan. Revelation 18:20 shares, "Rejoice over her, O heaven, and you holy apostles and prophets, for God has avenged you on her!"

We may struggle with this understanding now, but we can trust that God will transform our minds in heaven to perfectly reflect his thoughts in eternity. For now, our goal should be the same as the Lord, seeking to bring every person into faith with Jesus so others can experience eternal life.

78. ARE THERE LEVELS IN HEAVEN, AND IF SO, HOW DOES A PERSON REACH THEM?

The Bible clearly talks of heaven as the future home of the believer. However, many are curious concerning what heaven will be like. Some have even suggested there will be different levels in heaven. Is this true? And if so, how do we reach these higher levels?

Different levels of heaven are usually associated with ideas outside of the Bible. For example, the Mormon Church teaches three levels of heaven that include the celestial, terrestrial, and telestial kingdoms. Jehovah's Witnesses believe in a future heaven on a transformed earth, with a special area or level of heaven for one hundred forty-four thousand faithful witnesses. The popular classic narrative poem by Dante Alighieri (1265–1321) called *The Divine Comedy* includes nine levels of heaven.

However, the closest thing to levels in the Bible is found in a vision the apostle Paul experienced in 2 Corinthians 12. He spoke of a third heaven, which has caused many readers to ask questions about the identity of the first and second heavens.

In the Jewish understanding, the first heaven was the sky. In fact, in the Hebrew of the Old Testament and in the New Testament Greek language, sky and heaven are translated from the same word.

The second heaven was described as what we would call outer space. The stars, moon, sun, and other celestial objects exist in this second heaven.

The third heaven Paul described includes the spiritual realm where God lives with his people. Paul called it "Paradise" (2 Corinthians 12:4). In fact, in his vision he was not certain "whether in the body I do not know, or whether out of the body I do not know, God knows" (2 Corinthians 12:2). He only recorded that he had a vision of this heaven.

Instead of levels in heaven, the Bible speaks of different crowns or spiritual rewards believers will receive. Five different crowns are mentioned. They include the imperishable crown (1

Corinthians 9:24–25), the crown of rejoicing (1 Thessalonians 2:19), the crown of righteousness (2 Timothy 4:8), the crown of glory (1 Peter 5:4), and the crown of life (Revelation 2:10).

In Revelation 4:11, we read of the twenty-four elders who will lay their crowns down at the feet of Jesus, saying: "You are worthy, O Lord, to receive glory and honor and power; For You created all things, And by Your will they exist and were created." It does not appear these heavenly rewards will be a status symbol but rather an opportunity to enhance our worship of the Lord in eternity.

We do not need to worry about reaching a certain level of heaven because there are no levels with God. All believers will be in his presence for eternity. Instead, we are called both to believe and to faithfully serve him, knowing our actions matter, including crowns we can anticipate for faithful service.

79. WILL WE ASSOCIATE WITH ANGELS AND GOD IN HEAVEN?

The Bible teaches all believers will be with heaven for all eternity. God will be there, as will his angels. But what will our relationship with them be like? Will we interact with angels or with God in heaven?

When it comes to the Lord, we will certainly interact with him. Matthew 5:8 says the pure in heart will see God. Though we may not see God the Father or God the Spirit in visible form, we will certainly see the Lord Jesus Christ seated upon his throne.

In addition to seeing God, we will worship him. Revelation 5:13 includes every creature in heaven, people and angels, worshiping God together: "Blessing and honor and glory and power Be to Him who sits on the throne, And to the Lamb, forever and ever!" At least in this way, we will interact with angels and God at the same time.

Further, Isaiah 25:6 says will feast with the Lord in eternity: "And in this mountain The LORD of hosts will make for all people A feast of choice pieces, A feast of wines on the lees, Of fat things full of marrow, Of well-refined wines on the lees." Jesus affirmed this future feast, speaking of feasting in the kingdom of God (Matthew 8:11; Luke 22:30).

Luke 16:22 offers another interesting insight about the relationship between angels and people who will enter heaven. It reads, "So it was that the beggar died, and was carried by the angels to Abraham's bosom." This beggar, named Lazarus, was welcomed into God's presence with the assistance of angels. Though not specifically stated, it is likely we will enjoy a similar experience, with God's holy messengers accompanying us before the Lord upon the moment of death from this life.

Angels will also be present for those who go up to be with the Lord at the rapture. First Thessalonians 4:16 teaches, "For the Lord Himself will descend from heaven with a shout, with the voice of an archangel, and with the trumpet of God." An archangel will make an announcement, and other angels will likely be involved as well.

There is also one mysterious verse in 1 Corinthians 6:3: "Do you not know that we shall judge angels?" Paul mentions this question as a fact but does not elaborate. In some way, we will be involved in this aspect of the lives of at least some angels in heaven.

At the very least, it appears we will see angels in heaven and worship the Lord together. We will also eat or feast with the Lord. Beyond these areas, there may be much more we experience that the Bible does not describe. Even these limited insights into heaven should make us more excited about our future home with the Lord as we serve him today.

80. HOW DO WE KNOW GOD FORGIVES OUR PAST AND FUTURE SINS?

Jesus died for all our sins. First Corinthians 15:3 is clear on this point: "Christ died for our sins according to the Scriptures." But how can we know God has covered both our past and future sins?

Our past sins are forgiven the moment we come to faith in Jesus Christ. Colossians 2:13 teaches, "You, being dead in your trespasses and the uncircumcision of your flesh, He has made alive together with Him, having forgiven you all trespasses." Our "trespasses" are our sins. We like to remind people that all means all! There is no exception where you did something so bad in the past that God could not forgive your sin.

But what about future sins? We are called to live holy lives as believers and to flee from sin. However, we continue to make mistakes and sin as we live for God. When we do, we are taught to confess these sins to the Lord: "If we confess our sins, He is faithful and just to forgive us our sins and to cleanse us from all unrighteousness" (1 John 1:9).

Even though we are called to confess our sins, we are also promised eternal life as believers. This means even our future sins are covered. First John 5:13 declares, "These things I have written to you who believe in the name of the Son of God, that you may know that you have eternal life, and that you may continue to believe in the name of the Son of God." We have certainty about our future home with the Lord and his forgiveness of our sins.

However, we should not view God's mercy as an excuse to sin because he will forgive us for future wrongs. Romans 6:1–2 answers this question: "What shall we say then? Shall we continue in sin that grace may abound? Certainly not! How shall we who died to sin live any longer in it?" If we truly believe in Christ, we will not continue to desire sinning. Instead, we view ourselves as servants of Christ, seeking to obey his will for our lives.

Living in sin as a believer can hinder our prayers (1 Peter 3:7), our health (James 5:16), our relationships with other people (Galatians 5:15), and our witness to the lost. It is often through the example of our walk with God that others are drawn to know more about Jesus and come to faith through him.

Pastor Erwin Lutzer uses a wonderful illustration to highlight how God forgives our sins. He says to imagine two roads. One road is smooth and the other is rough and filled with bumps. When a heavy snow falls, both roads are covered with white and look the same. God does the same thing with our sins. We may view our sins as small or large, smooth or rough, but the forgiveness of Jesus covers all our sins white as snow. As Isaiah 1:18 reminds us, "Though your sins are like scarlet, They shall be as white as snow; Though they are red like crimson, They shall be as wool."

SECTION 10:

QUESTIONS ABOUT SEXUALITY AND GENDER

81. WHY DO CHRISTIANS SAY HOMOSEXUALITY IS A SIN?

In our culture, views of sexuality have increasingly changed in recent years. Even among many Christians, there is more acceptance of cultural views of sexual ethics, including same-sex activity. Many in our culture and churches ask: Why is homosexuality considered a sin?

The answer is found in two primary areas. The Bible holds a sexual ethic that excludes same-sex activity, and it often specifically calls same-sex activity sinful. Interestingly, the Bible does not specifically focus on sexual orientation, the concept that people are born with a desire for sexual relations with someone of the same gender or both genders. Instead, it emphasizes a sexual ethic limited to sexual activity between a man and woman within marriage.

First, let's look at the Bible's overall view of sexual ethics. Marriage was created by God as a lifelong relationship between one man and one woman (Genesis 2:24). In the Ten Commandments and elsewhere, adultery, or sexual activity outside of marriage, is condemned. This would include any same-sex activity—since same-sex marriage was not legal when God gave the law of Moses, any prohibition against sexual activity outside of marriage would by default prohibit same-sex activity. Even if the United States has made same-sex marriage legal, this change of law does not change the Bible's teaching on the subject. Though the Bible clearly includes examples of people who did not abide by these teachings, this does not change God's standard of sexual relations limited between one man and one woman within marriage.

Second, the Bible specifically condemns same-sex activity. In the Old Testament, many forms of sexual activity were condemned and were punishable by death under the law of Moses (Leviticus 18). In the New Testament, Jesus becomes the new covenant and believers are no longer bound by the law but by grace.

Some have erroneously argued this grace extends to same-sex relationships or even same-sex marriage, but this is an inaccurate interpretation of what Jesus and the New Testament teaches. For example, when Jesus was asked about divorce in Matthew 19, he affirmed the definition of marriage commanded in the garden of Eden in Genesis 2:24. He did not change or redefine marriage for other alternatives.

In addition, the New Testament lists same-sex activity as sinful in multiple places. In Romans 1:26–27 we read, "For this reason God gave them up to vile passions. For even their women exchanged the natural use for what is against nature. Likewise also the men, leaving the natural use of the woman, burned in their lust for one another, men with men committing what is shameful, and receiving in themselves the penalty of their error which was due." Both male and female same-sex relations are condemned as wrong.

A second mention is found in 1 Corinthians 6:9–10: "Do you not know that the unrighteous will not inherit the kingdom of God? Do not be deceived. Neither fornicators, nor idolaters, nor adulterers, nor homosexuals, nor sodomites, nor thieves, nor covetous, nor drunkards, nor revilers, nor extortioners will inherit the kingdom of God." The references to "nor homosexuals, nor sodomites" is translated in modern versions as one phrase, as they likely refer to the active and passive partners in male same-sex activity.

A third passage is found in 1 Timothy 1:9–10: "The law is not made for a righteous person, but for the lawless and insubordinate, for the ungodly and for sinners, for the unholy and profane, for murderers of fathers and murderers of mothers, for manslayers, for fornicators, for sodomites, for kidnappers, for liars, for perjurers, and if there is any other thing that is contrary to sound doctrine." The NIV and other modern versions translate "sodomites" as "those practicing homosexuality" to more specifically note the emphasis on same-sex actions.

Sexual sin of all kinds is a serious offense to God. Even the final chapter of the Bible warns in Revelation 22:15, "But outside are dogs and sorcerers and sexually immoral and murderers and idolaters, and whoever loves and practices a lie." Sexual immorality includes pre-marital sex, adultery, and same-sex activity as described throughout the Bible.

God's standards for sexuality are much different than those of our culture. Believers are called to live single and celibate or to marry one person of the opposite gender and remain sexually faithful to that person (1 Corinthians 7). All other forms of sexual activity are immoral and sinful and must be avoided by those who seek to faithfully follow the Lord.

82. IS ALL SEX BEFORE MARRIAGE A SIN? WHAT IF THE PEOPLE LOVE EACH OTHER AND ARE PLANNING TO MARRY?

Today's statistics note 40 percent of children in America are born into single-parent homes.[9] In addition, 35 percent of unmarried parents are cohabitating. Our sexual choices have consequences, including pregnancy. Perhaps this is why God's teachings regarding sexual activity outside of marriage between a man and woman are much more restrictive than what our society permits and even encourages.

In the Old Testament, the law of Moses taught that a person was to remain a virgin until marriage. Within marriage, adultery or other sexual activity was also prohibited under penalty of death. In the New Testament, Jesus affirmed the original definition of marriage as God gave in the garden of Eden (Genesis 2:24; Matthew 19:1–10).

In 1 Corinthians 6:16–20 we are offered the most direct teaching about sexual purity outside of marriage: "Do you not know that he who is joined to a harlot is one body with her? For 'the two,' He says, 'shall become one flesh.' But he who is

9   Gretchen Livingston, "The Changing Profile of Unmarried Parents," Pew Research, April 25, 2018, https://www.pewresearch.org/social-trends/2018/04/25/the-changing-profile-of-unmarried-parents/.

joined to the Lord is one spirit with Him. Flee sexual immorality. Every sin that a man does is outside the body, but he who commits sexual immorality sins against his own body. Or do you not know that your body is the temple of the Holy Spirit who is in you, whom you have from God, and you are not your own? For you were bought at a price; therefore glorify God in your body and in your spirit, which are God's."

These verses emphasize sexual purity outside of marriage. Yet some ask whether premarital sex is acceptable in certain cases, such as when a couple is engaged or plans to marry. While our society sometimes causes temptations through prolonged engagements or encouraging marriage later in life, this does not change the Bible's teachings in this area. Engagement is not marriage and does not make pre-marital sexual activity God-approved.

The overall biblical teachings regarding sexuality command that sex is for marriage. There is no exception because "we really love each other" or a couple wants to live together before marriage. These and other attempts to find an exception are based on feelings rather than the explicit teachings of Scripture.

Instead of seeking ways to redefine biblical teachings in this area, Scripture encourages us to focus on living fully for God. While marriage is a wonderful thing, compromising our sexual standards before marriage is not. When we place God as the top priority in our lives, we will choose his way.

The biblical example of Joseph remains powerful still today. He was asked to sexually compromise with the wife of his master. He refused and was wrongfully punished for it. Yet God later intervened and honored Joseph with a life and legacy that impacts many still today. Let's keep our standards high and honor God in our sexual ethics.

83. DOES THE BIBLE ADDRESS TRANSGENDERISM?

Transgenderism and gender identity issues have become controversial social topics in recent years. Does the Bible address this sensitive subject?

While there are no direct transgender verses in Scripture, the Bible does deal with the issue. Several important principles can be noted. First, God created people as one of two genders, male or female. Genesis 1:27 states, "So God created man in His own image; in the image of God He created him; male and female He created them." There was not a third gender, and certainly not fifty or more genders as some groups claim today.

Second, the transgender movement often blurs the distinction of two main areas. First, there are people born with abnormalities regarding their male or female body parts. Second, there are many other people who identify as transgender who are biologically male or female yet choose to live as a different gender.

In the case of those born with physical differences, we are called to offer much compassion with these medical issues. As to the many others who seek to live as a person of another gender or even medically alter their bodies to appear as another gender, biblical teachings instruct them to think and live differently.

The Bible does not call us to attempt to change our physical gender or identity but calls us to find our identity in Jesus

Christ. When we receive him and believe in him, we become his children, his sons and daughters (John 1:12). We become a new creation in Christ: "If anyone is in Christ, he is a new creation; old things have passed away; behold, all things have become new" (2 Corinthians 5:17).

God himself serves as our heavenly Father. Instead of seeking our identity through a different gender, we can accept ourselves as children of God, adopted by him for all eternity (1 John 3:1). Even as believers in Jesus, we may deal with thoughts and desires that are not from God, but this does not change our biological gender nor our identity in Christ.

Even the apostle Paul spoke of being tempted toward things he knew he was not intended to do. When this happened, he wrote of disciplining his body to do what was right: "I discipline my body and bring it into subjection, lest, when I have preached to others, I myself should become disqualified" (1 Corinthians 9:27). We may have feelings toward certain areas outside of God's plan for our lives, but we do not have to be controlled by these desires.

A person who struggles with his or her gender identity should not be mocked or ridiculed by Christians, which has sadly often been the case. Every person is a unique creation of God and is loved by him. We are called to show love to all people, helping others embrace God's message of hope found in a new life with Jesus Christ.

84. Is it right or wrong for churches to perform same-sex weddings?

The legalization of same-sex marriage in our country has led to the new challenge of churches being forced to decide whether it is right or wrong to perform same-sex weddings, as well as related matters of allowing church facilities to permit same-sex ceremonies even if performed by other groups.

First, as of the time of this writing, churches are not legally required to allow their church property to be used for same-sex weddings or to perform them. The First Amendment grants the free exercise of religion, including ministerial exceptions to performing services that are against their religious convictions.

Second, the Bible teaches against same-sex relationships, which would include supporting same-sex weddings (see our question on what the Bible teaches regarding homosexuality). Because we are called to oppose same-sex activity as followers of Christ, we certainly should not perform same-sex weddings.

Third, some have attempted to use Scripture to support so-called marriage equality and encourage churches to support same-sex marriage. For example, 1 Corinthians 7:9 has been used to support same-sex marriage because it says, "If they cannot exercise self-control, let them marry. For it is better to marry than to burn with passion." However, this verse is addressed to believers in the context of traditional marriage, with Paul encouraging either singleness or marriage between one believing man and one believing woman.

Fourth, what about churches or denominations that have changed their view regarding LGBTQ issues? If the church has embraced this new "inclusive" view, shouldn't a church and its ministers be able to conduct same-sex marriage ceremonies?

The biblical answer is, again, no. Legally, the answer is yes, but this does not change the Bible's teachings in the area. In fact, we would argue that if your church has embraced same-sex relationships or marriage as biblically acceptable, you should find another church. Scripture is unchanged in this area, despite compromises by major denominations and church leaders on this issue.

In addition, due to ongoing legal challenges in this area, we would recommend every church updates its policies to explicitly state its convictions regarding same-sex marriage and related matters. This topic can be much better addressed in any future controversy if it is a documented part of a church's constitution, statement of faith, and membership teaching. Christian legal groups are available to help provide guidance in this area if needed.

Hebrews 13:4 is helpful in this discussion as well. It teaches, "Marriage should be honored by all, and the marriage bed kept pure" (NIV). In the church, we are called to protect marriage, to honor it, and to encourage marriage purity. Marriage between a believing man and woman is God's plan and should be ours as well. We cannot change God's teachings, nor do we need to do so.

Psalm 19:10–11 remind us of the value of applying God's Word in all areas of life: "More to be desired are they than gold, Yea, than much fine gold; Sweeter also than honey and the honeycomb. Moreover by them Your servant is warned, and in keeping them there is great reward." God's truth is sweet and brings reward. Let us not change from it to appear contemporary or relevant, but rather let us remain faithful and experience God's rewards in eternity.

85. SHOULD I ATTEND A SAME-SEX WEDDING?

A generation ago, the question of whether to attend a same-sex wedding did not exist. Such a union was not even allowed by federal law until 2015. Many Christians are unequipped regarding how to respond to an invitation to a same-sex wedding, and the Bible was certainly not written during a time when such relationships were legal. Should we attend a same-sex wedding?

Though the Bible was written in a time before the legalization of same-sex marriage, it does provide irrefutable teaching on this issue. First, the New Testament says that same-sex relationships are immoral and are not to be part of our lives as followers of Jesus. Romans 1:26–27 teaches, "For this reason God gave them up to vile passions. For even their women exchanged the natural use for what is against nature. Likewise also the men, leaving the natural use of the woman, burned in their lust for one another, men with men committing what is shameful, and receiving in themselves the penalty of their error which was due."

But what about a friend or family member who is involved in a same-sex wedding? Scripture also pronounces that we are to focus on what is good and right: "Finally, brethren, whatever things are true, whatever things are noble, whatever things are just, whatever things are pure, whatever things are lovely, whatever things are of good report, if there is any virtue and if there is anything praiseworthy—meditate on these things" (Philippians 4:8). Supporting a same-sex wedding through our attendance would give attention to something that is not pure or just according to God's Word.

While no sin is greater than another in Scripture, we would advise against attending a same-sex wedding of a friend or loved one. Doing so appears to condone or support the union, even if you clearly note your concerns with it.

If we ask ourselves, *Would Jesus attend a same-sex wedding if he lived on earth today?* We would argue he would not. If he would not do so, why would we? We are called to conform to the image of Christ (Romans 12:1–2), living in the world without being of it. We must even do so when others oppose our biblical beliefs, knowing, "If the world hates you, you know that it hated Me before it hated you" (John 15:18).

Instead, we are to pray for those involved in such relationships and seek to show the love and teachings of Christ to those who live differently. Just as Christ lived to seek and save the lost, we are also called to bring God's message to those around us. We do not need to resort to hate or resentment toward a loved one in a same-sex relationship or marriage, but we must show God's compassion even when it is difficult to do so.

When we do, we remain firm in our convictions and show consideration to those who believe differently. We cannot make another person change his or her view, but we can set an example through our beliefs and actions in a way that is respectful yet courageous.

SECTION 11:

QUESTIONS ABOUT CHURCH AND CHRISTIAN LIVING

86. WHAT SHOULD I LOOK FOR IN A CHURCH TO ATTEND?

With more than three hundred twenty thousand churches in America, how can we decide which one to choose? This is a common question we have been asked many times. While each person must choose the best church God leads them to, there are some areas to consider when making such an important decision.

First, look at the church's statement of faith. Does the church hold to the Bible as the inspired Word of God? Is salvation clearly by grace through faith in Christ, without additions such as baptism, church membership, or expressing certain spiritual gifts? What does the church believe about the Trinity, Jesus, and even marriage and family?

Second, look at the church's leadership. How long have the key leaders served in the church? What is the reputation of the church's leaders? What do they emphasize?

Third, consider the church's ministries. If you have young children, this area of ministry will be important. If you are a single parent, is there anything specific to help you? What ministries exist for senior adults, teenagers, college students, men, or women?

Fourth, look at the church's recent sermons or services. If the church's services are online, take time to see what they sing and preach. Is the emphasis on honoring God? Does the pastor preach from the Bible? No church is perfect, but a healthy church will reflect honor of God in its worship services.

Fifth, what is the church's focus on outreach and missions? Remember, the mission of the church is the Great Commission. Is the church involved in reaching those in its community? Is there a list of upcoming mission trips or missionaries the church supports?

Sixth, research the church's history. How long has it existed in the community? What is its reputation? Who do they reach locally? A church with a strong history is positive sign. However, a newer church with less history may also be an open door to join a recently launched ministry to impact new lives.

Seventh, what is the church's diversity? Does the congregation reflect the surrounding community? Is there an effort to reach those from different backgrounds? Though reaching those of different ethnic groups presents a challenge to most churches, healthy churches are at least attempting to help serve the people of a variety of backgrounds near their congregation.

Consider also what Jesus said about his followers: "By this all will know that you are My disciples, if you have love for one another" (John 13:35). A church known for its love is a church that will attract those seeking new life. A healthy church should also reflect the same essentials as the first church. Acts 2:42 noted, "They continued steadfastly in the apostles' doctrine and fellowship, in the breaking of bread, and in prayers." A church focused on God's Word, relationships, worship, and prayer is a church to seriously consider joining.

There is no perfect church, but a growing, healthy congregation will be one with biblical theology, strong leadership, ministries to reach a variety of needs, and a focus on impacting the community and world.

87. WHY ARE THERE SO MANY DENOMINATIONS?

Christianity has developed into thousands of denominations worldwide. While this may sound divisive and negative, denominations form for a variety of reasons, with some that are negative and others that are positive.

Prior to the 1500s, the two major branches of Christianity included the Roman Catholic Church and the Orthodox Church, with the major difference involving the leadership of the Catholic Church by the pope. The Protestant Reformation, led by Martin Luther, resulted in the development of new groups of churches independent of the Catholic Church based on the Word of God and salvation by faith alone. The three major church movements included the Lutheran Church, the Presbyterian Church (largely influenced by John Calvin), and

Anabaptist or free churches, led by Huldrych Zwingli and focused on the practice of believer's baptism by immersion.

From these branches of Protestant church have come a wide variety of groups. Some other well-known denominations in the United States include Methodists (formed under John Wesley's leadership), Baptists (of various subgroups), the Assemblies of God, the Evangelical Free Church, Nazarene Church, and many others.

Some of these groups formed based on regions, such as Southern Baptists that began in the southern part of the United States. Other groups started based on various distinctives, such as the numerous charismatic churches of the twentieth century started under the influence of practicing charismatic gifts. More recently, non-denominational churches have increased in popularity, as new churches have sought to avoid the divisions or negative reputations of some past denominations.

Positive reasons for new denominations have included the starting of new churches in growing areas as well as new denominations started when churches have left previous groups with unbiblical theology. Negative reasons for denominations have included splits or divisions based on leaders who have had integrity issues as well as denominations divided over theological issues, such as no longer believing in the Bible is the inspired Word of God.

Denominations can offer great advantages when managed well. As a group, several churches working together as a denomination can better fund missionary work to unreached people. In addition, a denomination of churches can bring unity by standing for key biblical issues in culture, such as supporting the pro-life movement or standing for religious freedom.

However, denominations have often been viewed negatively, showing disunity in the body of Christ. This has sometimes sadly been true, as too many churches, leaders, and members have chosen to divide and start new groups rather than reconcile with current ones. Instead of viewing denominations positively or negatively, however, we encourage believers to evaluate each independent congregation.

The local church usually operates best at the local level, offering hope to those in its community. When we look at the division in today's denominations, we can easily become discouraged. However, when we seek ways to get involved in a local church and serve, we can make a great impact on others and lead others to faith in Christ.

In John 17:20–21, Jesus prayed, "I do not pray for these alone, but also for those who will believe in Me through their word; that they all may be one, as You, Father, are in Me, and I in You; that they also may be one in Us, that the world may believe that You sent Me." He desires unity among his people. Our goal must be to work together with other believers on the foundations of God's Word to make disciples of all nations.

88. WHAT DOES THE BIBLE TEACH ABOUT WOMEN IN CHURCH LEADERSHIP?

One of the most controversial areas of church teaching today involves the role of women in leadership. What does the Bible teach on this important topic?

First, Scripture tells us that both men and women are made in God's image and are equal in value to him. Genesis

1:27 says, "God created man in His own image; in the image of God He created him; male and female He created them." The question is not about the worth of a man or a woman but the role of men and women in local church congregations.

Second, Scripture offers two key local church leadership roles, elders (also called bishops or pastors) and deacons. First Timothy 3 provides the qualifications for both roles, while Titus 1 repeats the roles of an elder stated in 1 Timothy.

Third, a look at these leadership qualifications should be what determines how men and women lead in the church. While some suggest these leadership roles or definitions only applied in New Testament times and not today, there is no indication in Scripture for making this change. Instead, these qualifications appear to apply both to the time they were written as well as today.

In describing the qualifications for elders in 1 Timothy 3 and Titus 1, the text clearly uses male pronouns and speaks directly to men. This is also made evident by the requirement for an elder to be "the husband of one wife" (1 Timothy 3:2; Titus 1:6). At the very least, Paul's letters indicate only men were to serve as the elders overseeing each local congregation.

In addition, 1 Timothy 3:8–13 provides qualifications for deacons. Their traits are nearly identical to those for elders, with the exception that elders had to be "able to teach." Verses 8–11 are undoubtedly written to men.

Verses 12–13, however, use the Greek word translated "women" or "wives." This has traditionally been understood as referring to the wives of deacons and most likely does. However, some have understood these verses as a teaching for female deacons. Because the text is not completely certain, some churches and denominations allow for both male and female deacons in their congregations.

So how should churches apply these teachings today? At a minimum, a local church should include male leadership equivalent to the elder role that is responsible for the church's teachings. Some would limit this to the senior pastor (in a church with only one pastor), while others apply it to all pastoral positions.

Deacons are a more controversial topic since the Scriptures regarding whether they are male or male and female are not as clear. Each church or denomination must determine how to apply these verses and handle them accordingly. Some churches do not even have an official group of deacons, viewing deacons (a word meaning "servants") as an unofficial role in the church.

Other than these roles, Scripture offers a wide variety of leadership opportunities for women in ministry that culture often limits. Jesus personally held a high view of women in his ministry and offers an example for the church in this area. Both men and women are called to serve and complement one another in serving the church and making disciples as part of their unique gifting in the body of Christ.

89. HOW CAN I KNOW GOD'S WILL FOR MY LIFE?

Knowing God's will for your life is a vital part of faithful service to the Lord. Yet we often meet people who struggle to understand how God would have them live. How can we better know the will of God for our lives?

First, God provides many specific ways he wants us to live in his Word. For example, we do need to debate whether we should pray or attend church or help those in need. These are clear commands of Scripture. A life focused on regular Bible study is part of God's will for every believer.

Second, God's will for us includes prayer. It has been said a prayerless life is a meaningless life. Why? Because we cannot know God's will if we do not communicate with him.

Third, as believers we have God's Spirit living in us to guide us toward his will. If we are praying, studying God's Word, and obeying what we know is true, we can more easily hear from God's Spirit regarding the specific decisions God desires for our lives.

In addition to these essentials, we often desire to know specific information, like which career should I pursue? Whom should I marry? Where should I live? Should I go on this particular mission trip? While we would like a text message from God to tell us these answers, he often answers in other ways.

One of these ways is God's providence. Also called "circumstances," the Lord often allows our lives to be directed in a manner that makes one choice obvious over others. For example, you may be considering two different choices of employment. As you pray, God may reveal one company will allow you to have Sundays free to be involved in your church while the other would not. This circumstance may be the information needed to help confirm God's decision.

Another way God sometimes answers is through community. As we pray and seek God's solution, he will often speak through the godly advice of other believers. When making a major decision, don't be afraid to discuss it with trusted

Christian friends for help. God may make your answer clear through this process.

A third way God sometimes answers is through timing. When God answers a prayer in a clear and obvious way at a particular time, he's trying to communicate with us. We don't have to always seek out a supernatural timing for his answer but can be thankful when God does offer clarity through the timing certain events occur.

A final way God sometimes answers is through supernatural events. Though these are often difficult to evaluate, the Bible is filled with visions, dreams, miracles, healings, and other supernatural methods the Lord sometimes uses to provide an answer to his will for our lives. We cannot plan for these events, but we must not rule out when God works in unexplained ways.

God's will involves living for him each moment to better hear when he communicates. We may not always hear from him at the time or in the way we want, but he answers according to his perfect will to show us the next steps in our lives.

90. WHAT DOES THE BIBLE TEACH ABOUT DIVORCE AND REMARRIAGE?

One of the most difficult issues facing our culture is divorce. While we desire to uphold what God's Word teaches on the subject, we realize this is much more than finding textbook answers. We are dealing with life's closest relationships, often involving children in ways that impact their entire lives. Because of the serious nature of divorce, we must carefully consider God's principles and apply the truth in love in each context (Ephesians 4:15).

First, God's original design for marriage is one man and one woman in a lifetime relationship. Starting with Adam and Eve, we recognize this fundamental design for marriage while understanding that the ideal is not always what happens in our lives.

Second, the Bible does sometimes permit divorce. One clear example is found in Matthew 19:9: "I say to you, whoever divorces his wife, except for sexual immorality, and marries another, commits adultery; and whoever marries her who is divorced commits adultery." Adultery is the clearest biblical example given for allowing divorce (although the Bible does not require divorce in these cases).

Third, 1 Corinthians 7:15 says if an unbelieving spouse leaves, to let them go: "If the unbeliever departs, let him depart; a brother or a sister is not under bondage in such cases. But God has called us to peace." In some cases, even a person who claims to be a believer yet lives like an unbeliever may leave a marriage. We would recommend the same application in such a case.

Fourth, remarriage is sometimes encouraged. For example, 1 Corinthians 7:11 says a person who has divorced should remain unmarried or remarry their spouse. In addition, a person who is widowed through the death of a spouse can also remarry (1 Corinthians 7:39).

We should point out that the Bible does not directly answer every marital situation. It provides guidelines but not exact details. For example, if a believing spouse leaves, can he or she remarry another believer? This seems to be true but is not specifically stated, leaving people with a variety of views on the issue.

Another disturbing area involves a spouse who has been abused. The Bible does not directly say a woman should divorce a man who is abusive, but what would Jesus say to this issue? He certainly would not tell a woman and her children to remain in such a danger. At the very least, she should separate from an abusive spouse for safety. It would seem right to also allow divorce in such cases since the abusive spouse is not acting as a believer.

In all cases, believers are called to care for those in need. Many people contemplating or enduring divorce need the support of Christians friends, yet this is the time many believers fail to help. We must seek to help families in whatever way we can, offering the love of Christ in every circumstance.

91. What is a Christian view of the issue of abortion?

What should Christians believe about abortion? Though the modern practice of ending a child's life in the womb is not in the Bible, Scripture offers much evidence to support a pro-life view.

First, God declares the value of all human life in Genesis 1:27: "God created man in His own image; in the image of God He created him; male and female He created them." God makes every life in his image, with great value, care, and love.

Second, God defines the baby in the womb as a child. For example, when Mary visited her relative Elizabeth, we read, "And it happened, when Elizabeth heard the greeting of Mary, that the babe leaped in her womb; and Elizabeth was filled with the Holy

Spirit" (Luke 1:41). The same word for "babe" is used in Greek for the child in the womb as when a baby is out of the womb.

Third, God forms each person as a child from the womb. In Psalm 139:13, the psalmist rejoices, "You formed my inward parts; You covered me in my mother's womb." God's shows his care in the making of each human life far before a child leaves his or her mother's womb.

Fourth, God creates each person with a purpose from the point of conception. In Jeremiah 1:5, God told the prophet, "Before I formed you in the womb I knew you; Before you were born I sanctified you; I ordained you a prophet to the nations." Jeremiah had been set apart with a purpose even before God formed him in the womb. This affirms the value of life from the point of conception.

Fifth, even the Old Testament law revealed the equality of the child in the womb with a child out of the womb. In Exodus 21:22–25, the punishment for causing the death of an unborn child was death, just as it was for the murder of a person out of the womb.

But what about difficult situations such as a child conceived through rape or when there could be risk to the health of a mother? Let us be clear: we believe God always values life—despite the circumstances or even the potential disabilities of the child. We must seek the protection of life as top priority even when the situation is incredibly difficult.

However, it is also noted that less than two percent of America's abortions are due to such circumstances. This means more than 98 percent of all abortions could be stopped today even if these extreme cases were not included, saving millions of young lives.

Despite these and other teachings supporting the lives of the unborn, many, including entire denominations, affirm the woman's so-called right to choose. Since the legalization of abortion in 1973, more than sixty-two million children have been aborted. This is ten times the number of Jews killed in the Holocaust under Nazi Germany!

As believers, we are called to speak for those who cannot speak for themselves (Proverbs 31:8). This certainly includes the lives of the unborn. We must not only understand the Bible's pro-life teachings, but we called to do our part to protect the lives of the unborn as we are able.

92. DOES THE BIBLE SAY ANYTHING ABOUT CREMATION?

Sometimes people ask us what the Bible teaches about cremation. The practice has become more common in our society as a more affordable burial alternative and has been popularized through the cremation in eastern religious practices. What does the Bible teach about cremation?

A close look at the Old Testament reveals burial was the traditional custom. Because Israel was a rocky, hardened land, tombs were created in caves where bodies were wrapped and placed to rest. In many cases, the body would later have its bones placed in a bone box called an "ossuary." The only known Old Testament example of burning a dead body is found in 1 Samuel 31:11–13. Saul and his sons had been killed in battle, and the bodies were burned before the bones were buried. This followed the practice of burying the bones of a person to keep animals from destroying their remains.

The early church included many Jews who continued to follow these practices. Judaism still opposes cremation today, but this is based on tradition rather than direct biblical teachings. Scripture reminds us that the body decays and returns to dust. At the coming of Jesus, the dead in Christ will rise first and be given new glorified bodies regardless of the condition in which their current bodies were buried (1 Corinthians 15:51–58; 1 Thessalonians 4:13–18).

The Bible makes no command regarding whether a person should be cremated or buried in some other way. Some Christians oppose cremation because it is a practice associated with Hinduism, but this does not mean it is wrong for a Christian to be cremated.

Even so, some Christian traditions officially oppose cremation. For example, Greek and Russian Orthodox churches teach against cremation. The Roman Catholic Church teaches that it prefers traditional burial but permits cremation. Most Protestant churches do not oppose cremation as they emphasize a believer's soul going to be with the Lord and see no biblical passage specifically opposing the practice.

However, we do offer one word of caution. Sometimes a person desires to have their ashes spread or poured out in a unique way, such as into a lake or river in some symbolic action. This is not recommended as it follows the eastern religious idea of reincarnation, emphasizing a person's life returning the earth and coming back in another form. Though not specifically prohibited in Scripture, it appears to reflect an idea Christians do not want to communicate. Instead, a Christian's body is laid to rest to honor a person's life. This act also provides a physical place where loved ones can come to mourn and remember their departed loved one.

Instead of focusing on how a person is buried, the Bible emphasizes our glorious future with the Lord in eternity. Our body will decay, but our soul will live forever with the Lord as believers. Whether a person chooses cremation or traditional burial is a matter of preference. So long as loved ones seek to honor God in commemorating a person's life, either form of burial is acceptable.

SECTION 12:

QUESTIONS ABOUT THE END TIMES

93. IS THE ANTICHRIST ALIVE NOW?

The Antichrist is a future world ruler who will control the kingdoms of the earth and persecute Christians during the tribulation period. But many wonder when this Antichrist will appear. Is he alive today?

Daniel 9:26 calls the Antichrist "the prince who is to come," while 2 Thessalonians 2:3 (NIV) calls him a man of lawlessness and son of destruction. Whoever this individual is, he will be a global leader known for lawbreaking, deception, and destruction.

The word Antichrist is found four times in the New Testament (1 John 2:18, 22; 4:3; 2 John 1:7). He will be a person who denies Christ, with John noting many antichrists in his own time. The work of the Antichrist is mainly mentioned in Daniel 7–12, in 2 Thessalonians 2, and in Revelation 13, with the chapter in Revelation as the main passage addressing his identity and work.

In Revelation 13, this Antichrist is clearly male. Daniel describes him as coming from the revived Roman Empire. He will be someone who seeks to unite religions yet holds to none. He will deceive many, ultimately commanding others to worship him.

Whether a person holds the view that the rapture will occur before the seven-year tribulation or after, we must recognize this Antichrist could be alive today. For those who believe Jesus will return for his people before the tribulation, the Antichrist will arise after this any-moment event to confirm a seven-year peace agreement with Israel. Those who interpret Jesus returning at the end of the tribulation could also see the Antichrist active at any time as his efforts could already be in action headed toward Christ's future return.

As believers, we don't need to fear the future Antichrist, but we should be alert for any person who denies Christ, and we can be prepared for the persecutions that will accompany his time in power. The main difference is that the future Antichrist will eventually become a global leader out of modern Europe who will form a peace agreement with Israel. Anyone fitting this description could potentially fit in the role of the coming Antichrist, though Revelation 13 describes additional characteristics of his leadership.

Two important aspects noted there include his rise from a mortal wound and the mark of the beast. The Antichrist will appear to have died but will return to strength. In addition, he will force all people under his leadership to receive an unknown mark on their hand or head to buy and sell represented by the number 666.

He will be a man of war as well. His leadership will extend through the tribulation. Revelation 13:7 states, "It was granted to him to make war with the saints and to overcome them. And authority was given him over every tribe, tongue, and nation." His target will be those who believe in God, including persecuting Jews at that time.

We may not be able to identify the Antichrist today, but it is possible he is living. We need not live in fear of this future evil leader, but instead we are to focus on the true Christ as we await his future coming.

94. Do the issues in the Middle East today have anything to do with Bible prophecy?

With so much news activity in the Middle East, it is certainly reasonable to ask whether these events have anything to do with Bible prophecy. In some cases, we can make connections, but the Bible only occasionally refers to specific future events.

For example, the rebirth of Israel in 1948 is a clear fulfillment of predictions concerning the nation. In Ezekiel 34–39, the prophet predicted Israel would become a nation, return to the land from the nations of the world, and even use the Hebrew language again. These predictions have all been fulfilled in the past century.

In other cases, we can see events leading toward the fulfillment of future Bible prophecy. A good example is the war noted in Ezekiel 38. It describes lands in modern Russia, Iran, Turkey, and other nations in the Middle East coming together to attack Israel. These nations are increasingly united in hatred for Israel and often speak of attacks against the Jewish people. This prophecy has not been fulfilled yet but is certainly lining up with the Bible's predictions.

Another example can be seen in the general signs of our world. For example, increased globalism points toward a future time when the predicted Antichrist will lead the nations of the world. The push for peace in the Middle East and worldwide foreshadows a time when a false peace will be made with Israel for seven years. Even the push for a global cashless society seems to look toward a moment when commerce can be controlled by a mark similar to the mark of the beast in Revelation 13.

Two concerning examples observed today in the Middle East related to Bible prophecy are Christian persecution and anti-Semitism. Revelation 13:7 speaks of the Antichrist's attack on believers, something that continues to grow globally today. The Antichrist will also be known for his attacks on the Jewish people and for breaking a peace agreement with Israel. The rise of anti-Semitic acts and conflicts between Israel and Middle Eastern nations further point to future conflict.

Of great importance is the emphasis on Israel. In Bible prophecy, Israel is the nation that serves as God's centerpiece. Still today, this tiny nation receives an enormous amount of attention regarding events in the Middle East. In 2020, the nation was ranked the eighth most powerful in the world, despite being only the size of New Jersey and having been reborn as a nation for less than eighty years.

We should pay attention to events in the Middle East as they often relate to the ultimate fulfillment of Bible prophecy. However, the most important application of activity in the Middle East is to know Jesus and to live for him. Even if we don't completely understand the unfolding of prophetic events, we can know the Lord and be prepared for his future return.

95. WHAT IS AMERICA'S ROLE IN THE END TIMES?

One of the most common questions we hear concerning Bible prophecy is about America's role in the end times. However, many are unimpressed with our answer as the Bible does not seem to emphasize our nation's role in the last days.

First, the Bible predicts all nations will one day be under the control of a future Antichrist and will join in war against the Lord in Armageddon (Revelation 19). Yes, even America will one day serve as one of many nations in opposition to God.

Second, some see America as one of the nations opposing a future attack on Israel in Ezekiel 38. The reference in Ezekiel 38:13 to "the merchants of Tarshish, and all their young lions" may refer to western nations, including America. If so, it would fit the common response of many western nations today to oppose violence against Israel without getting involved to stop it.

Third, many believe the reason America is not emphasized in the end times will be due to many American Christians who will disappear at the rapture. Those who hold a pre-tribulation view of the rapture see America's role diminished during the tribulation as many in the nation will no longer be on earth during this time.

While this is certainly possible, there is no guarantee America's strength as a world leader will remain until the tribulation. Whether before the tribulation (due to external or internal problems) or during the tribulation (due to persecution or judgment), America and many nations will significantly weaken, leaving them powerless to overcome the Antichrist's leadership.

On the positive side, others see America playing a key role in connection with Israel in the last days. For example, the United States has led in the development of modern Israel and has even led in moving its embassy to Jerusalem as the capital of the nation. The recent Abraham Accords have also involved American leadership in normalizing relations between Israel and nations in the Middle East.

Though not directly mentioned, America may serve as part of helping Israel become a land of "unwalled villages" and "peaceful people" (Ezekiel 38:11) in the last days. If so, America will be part of blessing the land as described in Genesis 12:3.

Scripture's focus on Israel and surrounding nations remains the dominant theme of the end times, but America may have an important role. Individually, we are called to live for the Lord and share him with others as we look forward to that day (Hebrews 10:25).

96. WHAT DOES THE MARK OF THE BEAST MEAN?

The mysterious mark of the beast is described in Revelation 13:16–18: "It also forced all people, great and small, rich and poor, free and slave, to receive a mark on their right hands or on their foreheads, so that they could not buy or sell unless they had the mark, which is the name of the beast or the number of its name. This calls for wisdom. Let the person who has insight calculate the number of the beast, for it is the number of a man. That number is 666" (NIV). What does this mark mean?

This mark will include a mark on the head or right hand required for buying and selling. Though this mark predicts a future event, some see the foreshadowing of this mark in today's technologies. For example, the trend toward a cashless society could lead to purchases by a device a person could wear on the wrist or even by a tattoo or implant. Others have suggested an optical scan as consistent with a mark on the forehead.

In addition, the number is called "the number of a man." Who is the man, or who will he be? The number is related to a future global ruler. This mark will be connected to the future Antichrist. In New Testament times, coins had the image of the emperor on them. Today, American currency has the image of past presidents. The future mark of the beast will be consistent in this way, including some semblance of the future Antichrist who will serve as a global leader during the seven-year tribulation period.

Third, the mark of the beast will serve as part of an end-times deception. Revelation 13:14 adds, "Because of the signs it was given power to perform on behalf of the first beast, it deceived the inhabitants of the earth" (NIV). Those who take the mark will be people deceived by the Antichrist.

Fourth, the mark of the beast will serve as a form of allegiance to the Antichrist. As global leader, he will control commerce, buying, and selling. Those who have been tricked into believing he is the person who will bring world peace will be among those who take the mark.

Fifth, those who refuse the mark will be persecuted. Many Jews will likely refuse based on their faith in one God. Those who come to faith in Jesus during the tribulation will also refuse, recognizing the Antichrist as an evil end-times leader.

Some have attempted to connect the numerical values of the letters associated with 666 to Nero. Though uncertain, the connection would point toward the Antichrist as a future leader of the revived Roman Empire as Scripture predicts.

Regardless, we do not need to fear accidentally taking the mark of the beast today. We believe Jesus will come back at any moment, followed by the seven-year tribulation during which the mark of the beast will be implemented. Today's technologies may point to this future event but should not cause fear among believers living now.

97. DOES THE RAPTURE TAKE PLACE BEFORE OR AFTER THE TRIBULATION?

Bible teachers are often divided on the order of end time events. All Bible believing Christians agree Jesus is coming back at any moment to take his people to be with him but disagree regarding the timing.

Though many views exist, the two main views include the pretribulation view and posttribulation view. The pretribulation view teaches Jesus will come back at any moment to take his people to be with him prior to the start of the seven-year tribulation. This rapture is a separate event from the return of Jesus at the end of the tribulation where Jesus returns to earth with his people to defeat his enemies and begin his millennial reign.

The posttribulation view believes Jesus will only return once at the end of the seven-year tribulation. This view sees all Christian enduring the seven-year tribulation until Christ returns. Good arguments have been made for both views by devoted Bible teachers. However, we would conclude the pretribulation view is more likely for a variety of reasons.

First, the many differences between the rapture and the second coming passages are difficult to reconcile as one event. For example, the main rapture passages (1 Corinthians 15:51–58; 1 Thessalonians 4:13–18) describe Jesus taking the dead in Christ and living believers up to heaven with him. John 14 describes Jesus taking his followers to the Father's house in heaven. However, the second coming describes Jesus coming to earth with his followers to defeat his enemies. And this is just one of many differences.

Second, the pretribulation view makes the most sense of the church's absence in Revelation 4–18. Jesus gives letters to seven churches in Revelation 1–3, and believers later appear at the battle of Armageddon in Revelation 19. However, the church is not mentioned during the chapters of the tribulation. It seems the church is absent due to already being in heaven. Many Jews and some gentiles will still believe in Christ during the tribulation, but the rapture will have already occurred.

Third, the pretribulation view best fits the biblical teaching of Christ's any-moment return (also call imminence). If Christians are not taken to heaven until the end of the seven-year tribulation, an event that has not yet happened, it would be difficult to argue Jesus is coming back at any moment. Instead, the pretribulation rapture view emphasizes our need to live for Christ today as we may see him return literally at any moment.

This is why Paul concludes his discussion of the rapture in 1 Thessalonians 4:18 by telling believers to "comfort one another with these words." A posttribulation view does not comfort believers as we would endure seven years of persecution, the Antichrist, and the implementation of the mark of the beast. Instead, when we know Jesus is coming back at any moment for us prior to his judgment upon the earth, we can live with excitement about our future hope, knowing we will soon be in the presence of the Lord forever.

98. WHO IS MYSTERY BABYLON?

Revelation 17:5 describes a future mystery Babylon who will be judged in the last days: "On her forehead a name was written: MYSTERY, BABYLON THE GREAT, THE MOTHER OF HARLOTS AND OF THE ABOMINATIONS OF THE EARTH." Who is this mystery Babylon?

First, it is clear this is something that takes place during the future tribulation period. This mystery Babylon has not occurred yet but will be an important part of the last-days judgment of God. In fact, Revelation 17:3 reveals, "I saw a woman sitting on a scarlet beast which was full of names of blasphemy, having seven heads and ten horns." This beast was a reference to the Antichrist who will rule the Roman Empire revived in the last days.

Second, Revelation 17:9–10 describes mystery Babylon in the following way: "Here is the mind which has wisdom: The seven heads are seven mountains on which the woman sits. There are also seven kings. Five have fallen, one is, and the other has not yet come. And when he comes, he must continue a short time." Because of the reference to seven mountains resembling the seven hills of Rome known during the first century, the apostle John is most likely referring to the city of Rome.

Third, Revelation 17:18 ends the chapter by stating, "The woman whom you saw is that great city which reigns over the kings of the earth." The great city of the king is the capital of the revived Roman Empire in the last days. Since Rome was the capital of the original Roman Empire, the context is likely referring to Rome here as well. Some have even speculated the "woman" noted in this verse refers to the Roman Catholic Church or the "mystery" as referring to Catholicism. However, this is speculative and uncertain.

First Peter 5:13 is also helpful in identifying mystery Babylon. It says, "She who is in Babylon, elect together with you, greets you; and so does Mark my son." Scholars believe Peter was not in literal Babylon when he wrote these words but in Rome. The city was often referred to as Babylon in the first century because of its association of evil deeds.

But what about the view of mystery Babylon as the literal Babylon in the Middle East? Some have attempted to make this connection, especially when Saddam Hussein led Iraq and sought to rebuild the Babylonian ruins. While there may be a future role for this land, the mystery Babylon of Revelation appears to clearly emphasize Rome. In the last days, this city will serve as a center for the Antichrist's work yet will be judged by the Lord for its evil.

Others suggest the mystery of the whore of Babylon in Revelation 17 also includes the larger religious system in place during the last days. There may be some truth to this though the emphasis appears to be on the location the Lord will judge. Regardless, this mystery Babylon will rebel against the Lord and ultimately experience his judgment as part of Christ's second coming.

99. IS THE MILLENNIUM A LITERAL THOUSAND-YEAR REIGN?

Revelation 20:1–7 describes a future, one-thousand-year reign of Jesus on earth during a time called "the millennial kingdom." Will this be a literal thousand-year reign?

A straightforward reading of the passage reveals the term "one thousand years" used six times in these seven verses. It appears the apostle John specifically emphasizes this time as a literal versus a figurative period. Some suggest this number is figurative based on 2 Peter 3:8 that says, "Beloved, do not forget this one thing, that with the Lord one day is as a thousand years, and a thousand years as one day." While possible, the context of this verse is about Christ's patience in returning, offering as much time as possible for people to believe in the Lord.

This literal one-thousand-year period is also important for another reason. Other prophecies state that the Messiah, Jesus Christ, will rule as king in Jerusalem from David's throne. For example, Luke 1:31–32 reads, "Behold, you will conceive in your womb and bring forth a Son, and shall call His name Jesus. He will be great, and will be called the Son of the Highest; and the Lord God will give Him the throne of His father David."

The Lord's covenants included a descendant who would reign in the days to come in the promised land. In the Abrahamic covenant, God promised Abraham his descendants would reign (Genesis 12:1–3). He also promised David his descendants would establish his kingdom forever: "When your days are fulfilled and you rest with your fathers, I will set up your seed after you, who will come from your body, and I will establish his kingdom. He shall build a house for My name, and I will establish the throne of his kingdom forever" (2 Samuel 7:12–13).

In Zechariah 8:3, the Lord said, "I will return to Zion, And dwell in the midst of Jerusalem. Jerusalem shall be called the City of Truth, The Mountain of the LORD of hosts, The Holy Mountain." Though some see this as already fulfilled, the emphasis is on God personally leading from Jerusalem in the future, something that will take place when Jesus sits upon his throne in the millennial kingdom.

Another way to look at this issue is to ask whether there is any other option that makes better sense of the references to one thousand years. If this will not be a literal time period, then the only other option would be some kind of figurative or allegorical interpretation. However, the fulfilment of several predictions regarding the Messiah's future reign rightly finds its place if understood from the perspective of a future, literal millennial kingdom.

The best part is that at the end of the millennial kingdom, one final rebellion will take place. Jesus will quickly defeat and judge Satan and those with him (Revelation 20:7–15). This judgment will be followed by the creation of a new heaven and earth, including a new heavenly Jerusalem, where all of God's people will dwell with him for eternity (Revelation 21–22).

100. IF CHRISTIANS WILL GO TO THE NEW HEAVENS AND EARTH AT THE END OF TIME, WHERE DO THEY GO NOW AFTER DEATH?

The apostle Paul wrote that to be away from the body is to be present with the Lord (2 Corinthians 5:6–8; Philippians 1:23). Upon death, a believer instantly enters the presence of the Lord. But where will Christians be with God until the creation of the new heavens and earth in Revelation 21–22?

In John 14:1–3, Jesus speaks of leaving earth to go to the Father's house. He even says his followers will be with him also. The thief on the cross was told he would be with Jesus in paradise that day (Luke 23:43). In the account of the rich man and Lazarus, we are told Lazarus was taken by angels to Abraham's bosom (or side), indicating all believers in the Lord go to a place in the presence of the Father.

These biblical passages directly speak against the theory of some people called "soul sleep." According to this view, believers are simply on pause until Christ returns, at which point they join him in his future glory. Though the New Testament does speak of the death of believers as "sleep," this is not a reference to soul sleep but a kind way to describe a person's death. The person who knows the Lord finds rest at the end of this life, enjoying eternity with the Lord.

In Hebrews 4, the author also speaks of a future rest for the people of God. Verse 9 states, "There remains therefore a rest for the people of God." Verse 11 adds, "Let us therefore be diligent to enter that rest, lest anyone fall according to the same example of disobedience."

In fact, 1 Corinthians 15:50–54 and 1 Thessalonians 4:13–18 describe a future time known as the rapture when believers will be reunited with their new bodies. The dead in Christ will rise first followed by living believers, with all those in Christ receiving new bodies for future worship of the Lord.

Sadly, those who do not know the Lord will be eternally separated from him. Luke 16:22–23 describes the agony of the rich man in the afterlife apart from God. Following the future millennial kingdom, those judged at the great white throne judgment will be cast into the eternal lake of fire (Revelation 20:11–15). Even during the new heavens and new earth, we are reminded there will be those on the "outside" who will exist apart from the Lord.

At the end of the tribulation period, Jesus will return with all his people to defeat his enemies and reign in the millennial kingdom for one thousand years (Revelation 19–20). We will remain in the Lord's presence under his leadership in this kingdom until the creation of the new heavens and new earth described in Revelation 21–22.

Upon seeing his vision of this time, the apostle John wraps up the book of Revelation by declaring, "Amen. Even so, come, Lord Jesus!" (Revelation 22:20). As we learn about our future home, it should likewise encourage us regarding all we have to look forward to in eternity.

101. The Ultimate Question: Do you know for sure that you are going to heaven?

People everywhere invest their lives in the search for meaning, purpose, and fulfillment. But people need something more than money, fame, luxurious houses, good looks, nice cars, or a lucrative stock portfolio. There is nothing necessarily wrong with these things, but they cannot provide peace to the soul or forgiveness of one's sin.

I once read that the highest rates of suicide and divorce occur among the most affluent classes of society. On the West Coast, psychologists and counselors have isolated a new affliction and given it a name, "Sudden Acquired Wealth Syndrome." People are achieving every benchmark that our society says should make them happy, but they are finding that it is possible to be materially rich yet spiritually bankrupt. Many people have a schedule that is full but a heart that is empty.

Several years ago, our nine-member ministry team crossed America on a "50-States-in-50-Days" trip. During this journey to fifty states in fifty days, I preached in every service, in all fifty US states, and personally talked with thousands of people. We had the privilege of hosting sixty-four worship services throughout the entire United States. Our outreach team met many people who came to us with probing questions and genuine concern about spiritual issues. People today truly are looking for meaningful answers, craving hope in a dangerous world.

Present realities, such as worldwide terrorist attacks, global economic uncertainty, political instability, and natural disasters like hurricane Katrina and COVID-19 have only intensified this search.

Immediately after the terrorist attacks of 9/11, I went to New York City to help with a prayer center that had been set up by the Billy Graham ministry and Samaritan's Purse. Just like on my fifty-state tour, I was talking daily to hundreds of people from every background imaginable. They may have expressed themselves in different ways, but they all had the same basic question:

WHO IS GOD, AND HOW MAY I COME TO KNOW HIM?

Where one stands with God is the most vital of all issues, but the good news is that you may settle this today! You may have wondered, *How does a person become a Christian? How can I be certain that my sin is forgiven? How may I experience consistent spiritual growth?* Let's consider these things together.

GOD'S WORD EXPLAINS THE MESSAGE OF SALVATION

Jesus said in John 3:3, "No one can see the kingdom of God unless they are born again." Salvation is the issue: The most important question you will ever ask yourself is this: *Do I know for certain that I have eternal life, and that I will go to heaven when I die?*

If you stood before God right now, and God asked, "Why should I let you into my heaven?" what would you say?

The Bible describes our condition: "All have sinned and fall short of the glory of God" (Romans 3:23).[10] Just as a job pays a wage at the end of the week, our sins will yield a result at the end of a lifetime: "The wages of sin is death (the Bible describes this as separation from God, the punishment of hell), but the gift of God is eternal life, through Jesus Christ our Lord" (Romans 6:23).

God's love for you *personally* is shown by his provision for your need: "God demonstrates his own love for us in this: While we were still sinners, Christ died for us" (Romans 5:8).

Salvation requires repentance, which means a "turning." Jesus said, "Unless you repent, you too will all perish" (Luke 13:3). The New Testament emphasizes the necessity of repentance and salvation: "Repent, then, and turn to God, so that your sins may be wiped out" (Acts 3:19).

Every one of us has sinned, and the Bible says that our sins must be dealt with. We have a two-fold sin problem. We are sinners by birth, and we are sinners by choice. Somebody once said to Dr. Vance Havner, "This thing about man's sin nature, I find that hard to swallow." The great evangelist responded, "You don't have to swallow it—you're born with it; it's already in you."[11]

The world classifies sin, viewing some things as worse than others. But the Bible teaches that all sin is an offense against God, and even one sin is serious enough to keep someone out of heaven. You may not have robbed a bank, or maybe you have. God doesn't grade on a curve; humanity is a tainted race, and sin is the problem.

10   All verses in this section from the New International Version (NIV).
11   As noted in https://www.sbcevangelist.org/evangelists/everlasting-life/god-loves-you/, accessed March 25, 2021.

Oftentimes in life, we know what is right, but we do what is wrong. You may have even looked back at yourself and wondered, *What was I thinking? Why did I do that? How could I have said that?* Jesus said that man needs to repent and make a change. Repentance means turning *from* your sins and *to* Christ. By faith, trust *who* Jesus is (God's Son; mankind's Savior) and *what* Jesus did (died in your place and rose from the dead).

God's forgiveness is received by faith. We are to confess our faith before others, not ashamed to let the world know that we believe in Jesus: "If you declare with your mouth, 'Jesus is Lord,' and believe in your heart that God raised him from the dead, you will be saved. For it is with your heart that you believe and are justified, and it is with your mouth that you profess your faith and are saved" (Romans 10:9–10).

What is faith? Faith is trust. It is simple, honest, child-like trust. God says that you have a sin problem but that he loves you and will forgive you. God says that through Jesus Christ, he has made a way for anyone to be saved who will come to him. Do you trust what God has said, and what God has done? If you come to Christ in belief and faith, God promises to save you: "Everyone who calls on the name of the Lord will be saved" (Romans 10:13). Jesus promises: "Whoever comes to me I will never drive away" (John 6:37).

During the fifty-state tour, we gave away thousands of yellow stickers that said, "Jesus Saves, Pray Today!" That is not a trite saying or marketing cliché. It is a deep biblical truth, and if you desire to have a relationship to the Lord, that can be accomplished right where you are now. Make your journey to the cross today, through this basic prayer of commitment:

Dear Lord Jesus, I know that I have sinned, and I cannot save myself. I believe that you are the Son of God and that you died and rose again for me to forgive my sins and to be my Savior. I turn from my sins, and I ask you to forgive me. I receive you into my heart as my Lord and Savior. Jesus, thank you for saving me now. Help me to live the rest of my life for you. Amen.

God's Word Gives You Assurance of Salvation

You can overcome doubts about where you stand with God. Based on what God's Word says (not what you feel or assume), you can know that you have eternal life: "Whoever has the Son has life; whoever does not have the Son of God does not have life. I write these things to you who believe in the name of the Son of God so that you may know that you have eternal life" (1 John 5:12–13).

Jesus said, "Whoever hears my word and believes him who sent me has eternal life and will not be judged but has crossed over from death to life" (John 5:24). Remember: you are not saved by good works, and you are not "kept saved" by good works. Your merit before God is totally based on Jesus; his perfection, holiness, and righteousness are credited to each one who believes by faith.

WHAT IS MEANT BY THE TERM "REDEDICATION?"

A news reporter once asked me this question. He had heard me use this term as I spoke at a church, and he wanted to know what I meant. "Rededication" is for a believer who desires that their walk with Christ be renewed and deepened. A Christian can wander from God in sin or simply lose their closeness to the Lord through the business of life.

A born-again Christian is forever God's child. Your salvation is a matter of *sonship.* Your daily Christian growth is a matter of *fellowship.* Your spiritual birth into God's family is, in some ways, similar to your physical birth into the human family. For instance, in growing up as a child, you may have disobeyed and disappointed your father. Something you did may have grieved your father, but you were still his child because you had been born into that family.

In the same way, the Christian's relationship to the Lord is still intact even though a sin we commit may hinder our daily fellowship with God. Salvation is a one-time, instantaneous event; Christian growth and personal fellowship with God is an everyday, life-long process. Consistent daily prayer, Bible study, obedience to the Holy Spirit, and nurturing in a local church fellowship are all keys to growth and Christian maturity.

While your "sonship" may be intact, your daily "fellowship" may be lacking. Christ, not "self," must be on the throne of your heart and life! Sin hinders our fellowship with God. "But your iniquities have separated you from your God; your sins have hidden his face from you, so that he will not hear" (Isaiah 59:2). Perhaps your desire is like that of David, when he had wandered from God: "Create in me a pure heart, O God, and renew a steadfast spirit within me" (Psalm 51:10).

God lovingly receives all who *turn* to him and all who *return* to him. He cleanses us from sin and restores us to fellowship with him. King David had been "a man after [God's] own heart" (1 Samuel 13:14), but his sinful deeds required that he humbly re-commit himself to the Lord: "Do not cast me from your presence...Restore to me the joy of your salvation" (Psalm 51:11–12). Christian publications often use the following verse in the context of evangelism, and that is okay, but 1 John 1:9 is really a promise to the *Christian* who needs to make things right with the Lord: "If we confess our sins, he is faithful and just to forgive us our sins and purify us from all unrighteousness."

From the same chapter is another great truth that gives us precious, sweet assurance: "If we walk in the light, as he is in the light, we have fellowship one with another, and the blood of Jesus, his Son, purifies us from all sin" (1 John 1:7).

You may already know the Lord but wish to pray these basic words of rededication and commitment:

> *Lord Jesus, I acknowledge that I have sinned*
> *and wandered from you. I confess my sin and*
> *turn from it. I recommit myself to you as Lord.*
> *Thank you for forgiving me; I trust you to give*
> *me the strength to live for you each day of my*
> *life. Thank you for being my Savior, my Lord,*
> *and my friend. Amen.*

May God bless you as you journey on with him.

If you made a decision for Christ just now, it would be an honor to hear from you. If you do not have a Bible and would like to request one or if you have other questions or spiritual needs, write to:

Dr. Alex McFarland

c/o Truth for a New Generation

P.O. Box 10231

Greensboro, NC 27404

Or email us through the website at truthforanewgeneration.com or alexmcfarland.com.

ABOUT THE
AUTHORS

ALEX MCFARLAND is an evangelist, author, and advocate for Christian apologetics. Cohost of *Exploring the Word* with Bert Harper (heard nationally on the American Family Radio Network), Alex is the founder and president of the national apologetic conference *Truth for a New Generation*. He has served as president of Southern Evangelical Seminary and Director of Teen Apologetics for Focus on the Family under James Dobson. Alex currently directs Biblical Worldview for Charis Bible College. He has served as adjunct professor at several Christian universities, assisting with the creation of programs and departments dedicated to apologetics and defense of the Christian worldview. Alex is the author of many books, including the best-selling *10 Most Common Objections to Christianity*. He is a graduate of Liberty University. Alex and his wife Angela live in North Carolina.

BERT HARPER is the Director of Marriage, Family, and Pastoral Ministries at the American Family Association. He has served as cohost of *Exploring the Word* with Alex McFarland for more than a decade and is heard on an average of two hundred stations nationwide each weekday. As a pastor of local churches, Bert has nearly four decades of experience counseling couples. He has faithfully served on the Board of the American Family Association, Blue Mountain College, and in many other leadership roles on behalf of churches and Christian organizations. Together, he and his wife, Jan, lead marriage conferences and retreats for ministers and their wives. The Harpers have three grown sons and are the proud grandparents of a growing family.